Essays on Ecumenism

Essays on Ecumenism

✠ ✠ ✠

Leonidas C. Contos
Milton B. Efthimiou
Jeffrey Gros
Georges Tsetsis
Antoinette Wire
Methodios Fouyas

Compiled by
Anton C. Vrame, Ph.D.
and
Cory Dixon

InterOrthodox Press
Berkeley, California

Published by InterOrthodox Press
Patriarch Athenagoras Orthodox Institute
2311 Hearst Avenue
Berkeley, CA 94709

ISBN 1-932401-02-4

Library of Congress Cataloging-in-Publication Data
Essays on ecumenism / compiled by Anton C. Vrame and Cory C. Dixon.
  p. cm.
Includes bibliographical references.
 ISBN 1-932401-02-4 (pbk.)
 1. Christian union—Orthodox Eastern Church—Congresses. 2. Orthodox Eastern Church—Relations—Congresses. I. Vrame, Anton C. II. Dixon, Cory C., 1979-
 BX324.E83 2003
 281.9—dc22
                2003017167

Contents

Editor's Note

Over the last few years, the challenges within Orthodoxy about ecumenical dialogue, participation in the World Council of Churches and the various bilateral dialogues have made headlines in ecclesiastical circles. This phenomenon is surprising, because the Orthodox Church has been at the forefront of the Ecumenical Movement of the twentieth century. The Ecumenical Patriarchate's "Letter to the Churches of Christ Everywhere" in 1920 inaugurated the modern effort for rapprochement among the various Christian communions. His All Holiness Ecumenical Patriarch Athenagoras and his successors Dimitrios and Bartholomew follow a long tradition of dialogue.

The papers presented in this volume predate the headlines by just a few years. They reflect some of the issues that were causing consternation initially among Orthodox involved in ecumenical dialogue. The authors are some of the leading thinkers in ecumenical circles of the day. Their insights into issues are based in years of study and experience. Thus, they are presented here as a "snapshot" of Orthodox thinking in this period (1991-1993), as a record of the times, and to further dialogue among the Churches.

The first essay, "The Priesthood of the Laity" by Fr. Leon Contos, Alexander Spanos Professor of Eastern Orthodox Studies at the Graduate Theological Union, Berkeley, and a founder and president of the Patriarch Athenagoras Orthodox Institute was delivered as an address at a convocation of the Graduate Theological Union, October 3, 1991. That convocation awarded an honorary doctorate to His Eminence Archbishop Iakovos of North and South America.

The essay by Fr. Georges Tsetsis, representative of the Ecumenical Patriarchate to the World Council of Churches, was originally delivered as a talk at St. Vladimir's Orthodox Theological Seminary, Crestwood, New York on May 22, 1993.

"Orthodoxy and Ecumenism" by Fr. Milton Efthimiou, Ecumenical Officer of the Greek Orthodox Archdiocese of North and South America, was delivered at Holy Cross Greek Orthodox School of Theology, Bookline, Massachusetts on May 13, 1993.

On October 14, 1993, the Graduate Theological Union, the Ecumenical Ministries of Northern California and the Patriarch Athenagoras Orthodox Institute jointly sponsored a forum following the Fifth World Conference on Faith and Order held at Santiago de Compostela, Spain in August 1993. Presentations from that forum were made by Prof. Antoinette Wire of San Francisco Theological Seminary, Brother Jeffrey Gros from the Secretariat for Ecumenical and Interreligious Affairs of the National Conference of Catholic Bishops, and Fr. Milton Efthimiou.

The final three presentations were the Patriarch Athenagoras Orthodox Institute's Distinguished Lecture Series, held in February 1992. The lectures of His Eminence Metropolitan Methodios Fouyas of Pisidia dealt extensively with ecumenical topics from a historical, theological, and contemporary perspectives. He is well known for his critique of ecumenical dialogues even as an active participant in them. Thus including them in this volume is well suited.

Other than the presentations by Metropolitan Methodios, these essays were originally published in *Oikoumenika*, Occasional Papers Number 3 of the Patriarch Athenagoras Orthodox Institute. They are republished here so that they may receive wider attention. The essays were origially given as talks and lectures; thus they are quite diverse in their styles and levels of citation. We have not tried to "edit out" any inconsistencies in style or citations. Rather, we have kept each presentation intact, as it was presented originally, except to correct errors of a minor nature. My thanks go to Mr. Cory Dixon, a graduate student at The University of Chicago Divinity School for his painstaking efforts to prepare and check the manuscripts of each presentation.

Anton C. Vrame, Ph.D.
Editor

The Priesthood of the Laity

V. Rev. Leonidas Contos

This is the second time in the relatively short history of the Orthodox Institute that we have convened jointly with the Graduate Theological Union, our benevolent parent, in solemn but joyous assembly. In the winter of 1987 it was to inaugurate the newly endowed Chair in Orthodox Christian Studies, the first and thus far the only one in the country. It was also to dedicate the Institute under its new name, honoring, in the centennial year of his birth, the late great Patriarch Athenagoras. The dedicator that night was the very one the GTU honors this night with the highest academic dignity within its gift; again, the first and thus far only honorary degree ever voted by its trustees.

It was under the hand of Athenagoras that our honoree entered the holy priesthood. In turn the head of this Diocese, Bishop Anthony, a product of the same academic nurturing, was consecrated by him. Thus we have here, in the small as it were, the apostolic succession – visible, palpable, literal. From this little shard of history one might extrapolate that larger schema, wherein the ministry of the Church is held to derive from the Apostles in continuous and unbroken sequence.

This principle was emphasized before the end of the 1st century by Clement of Rome, although he refers to the "rulers" of the Church as bishops and presbyters without drawing a clear distinction between the two. And of course within the historic Church it has always been seen as indispensable. Most Reformation ecclesiology on the other hand has denied its necessity, in large part out of an underlying commitment to the priesthood of the laity.

I have set myself the impossible task of postulating within the span of a few minutes, that the gap between the two positions is not as unbridgeable as is commonly supposed. For while the Church has from earliest times known itself as hierarchical, it has also believed itself to be charismatic and pentecostal – in the biblical meaning. And while there is a special ordained priesthood, well articulated even in the 1st century into its three orders, the whole people of God possess gifts as prophets and priests, again in the biblical meaning. It may be that the charismatic ministries of healing, working miracles and speaking with tongues and the like (1 Cor. 12:28-30) are less in evidence – some will say, just as well; they make us uncomfortable – yet it would indeed be to "quench the Spirit and despise prophesying" (1 Thes. 5:20) if we were to say that they have been extinguished.

Moreover, in the Orthodox tradition of weaving Scripture and Liturgy into an existential unity, the testimony of St. Peter becomes part of the great Eucharistic Prayer in the Liturgy of St. Basil the Great: "He brought us to the knowledge of You, the true God and Father, redeeming us to Himself as a chosen race, a royal priesthood, a holy nation, God's 'own people.'" (1 Peter 2:9) (The Authorized Version reads "a peculiar people," and one must resist the temptation to engage in a commentary on that adjective.) For what purpose were we thus called out? – "That you may declare the wonderful deeds of him who called you out of darkness into his marvelous light."

In the special petition for the Bishop in the Liturgy, the essential note of his authority is that he be found "rightly proclaiming the word of thy truth." But the proclamation of the truth is not the same as the possession of the truth. All the people possess it; it is the bishop's special office to proclaim it publicly – always "rightly" always we must see him as "orthotomounta." There is no suggestion that he is himself infallible; infallibility belongs to the whole Church. As the Orthodox Patriarchs said in their letter to Pope Pius IX in 1848: "Among us neither Patriarchs nor Councils could ever introduce new teaching, for the guardian of religion is the very body of the Church, that is, the 'laos,' the people itself."

Alexei Khomiakov, the Russian philosopher-theologian, commenting on this statement, writes to his English friend W. J. Birkbeck: "The Pope is greatly mistaken in supposing that we consider the ecclesiastical hierarchy to be the guardian of dogma. The case is quite different. The unvarying constancy and unerring truth of Christian dogma does not depend upon any hierarchical order; it is guarded by the totality, by the whole people of the Church, which is the Body of Christ."

Central to Orthodox ecclesiology is the understanding that the authority of the bishop is the authority of the Church. However broad the prerogatives of his office may be, he is not someone set *over* the church, the preposition "epi" notwithstanding; he holds office *in* the Church. Bishop and people are united in an organic oneness, and neither can be thought of apart from the other. Very early in the 3rd century, Hippolytus, in the *Apostolic Tradition*, provides a detailed description of the rites and practices of that time. The twofold dimension of the bishop's office is explicit: he is God's representative to the ecclesia; but he is equally the ecclesia's representative before God. And this twofold representation requires a twofold authorization: from God and from the people. Any number of references can be adduced to demonstrate the importance attached to the bishop's free election in pre-Nicene times.

Thus it may be said that the "pleroma" of the Church, while it may not possess in any literal meaning the sacerdotal and the royal aspects of the priesthood that derives from Christ, certainly exercises the prophetic. I offer by way of illumination of this much–misunderstood aspect of the Orthodox tradition, these brief but compelling testimonies of history:

When, on the gloomy eve of Byzantium's tragic fall, its emperor and hierarchy signed the Act of Union at Florence, on terms that can only be described as humiliating, capitulating on the most fundamental of theological issues, largely at the insistence of Emperor John VIII, in the vain hope of securing in return Western aid against the Ottoman menace, it was in the end the people who repudiated the Union as an act of betrayal of the faith. ". . . The unerring truth of Christian dogma . . . is guarded by the . . . whole people of the Church."

Within a scant fourteen years the dark cloud of Islamic subjugation fell over the once magnificent city, dedicated by Constantine the Great, eleven centuries before, to the Holy Wisdom of Christ and to the Theotokos, spreading swiftly over all the Orthodox nations except Russia, now the "Third Rome," which saw it as the chastisement of history. For four hundred years the Great Church lived in captivity. Yet it lived. The faith was preserved. The Liturgy, often celebrated in secret as in Roman times, continued to sustain the "pleroma." The "kleronomia," the inheritance, including even the Greek language, taught furtively in caves and cellars by night, as the legends of the "Tourkokratia" so poignantly attest. Four centuries could not vanquish the conviction of a people that they constituted, even in the worst times, "a holy nation, a royal priesthood, God's peculiar people."

In Russia, where history has always recorded an ebb and

flow of religious enthusiasm, one thinks of the ministry of the "eldership," the "startsi," like St. Seraphim of Sarov, who exercised a spiritual influence on Russian intellectuals and peasants alike far greater than the institutional Church.

But let us come to our own century, indeed to history being lived and made. It is said that in the early stages of the Bolshevik revolution when concerned about the institution of the Church, Lenin dismissed it as an affair of little old ladies, "babushkas," the harmless grandmothers. In recent years, when the trickle of visitors from the outside entered the USSR, taking their Intourist guided excursions and eating their Intourist meals at Intourist hotels, the image persisted: that the churches, the few that functioned, were filled mainly with Babushkas. Few ever thought to ask: were these little grandmothers some sort of timeless avatars? Would they not have been little girls, or perhaps some of them even unborn, when Lenin so casually dismissed them as a force? And how did they reincarnate themselves through three generations, preserving that sacred faith and transmitting it, not without risk? Is this not again the priesthood of that people, in its most vital manifestation, standing guard at the repository of Sacred Tradition?

Pravda, which means "truth," failed in seventy years to nullify in the "totality of the people" the knowledge of and the yearning for authentic truth, that truth that sets one free. Out of the myriad television images chronicling the swift dissolution of one repressive communist regime after another, one that remains vivid for me is that of a lovely young woman in Bucharest saying, "We now have freedom, but we do not know what to do with it." In the light of truth it will be relearned.

I give you one last image, more recent, more personal. When the Ecumenical Patriarch visited America last summer,* there

---

*Editor's note: His All Holiness Ecumenical Patriarch Dimitrios visited the United States and Canada in July 1990.

was a moving moment in the serene intimacy of the Oval Office. The President spoke of the incredible changes happening before our very eyes, and he said to the Patriarch: all this stems from the faith of the people; for Orthodoxy this is a crucial time, to witness anew to the world to the timeless vitality of the living, and life-giving, faith.

This, in its simplest essence, is the task of the Patriarch Athenagoras Orthodox Institute, within the broad ecumenical enterprise of theological learning which is the Graduate Theological Union. In honoring the man who has borne this witness, as priest, and as priest of priests, for more than half a century, and who has from the very start given it his unstinting patronage, you honor our effort and our contribution, modest as it may be. For this our deep and abiding gratitude.

The Bilateral Dialogues of the Orthodox Church
(Problems and Opportunities)

V. Rev. Georges Tsetsis

As a result of decisions taken by the Second and Third Pan-Orthodox Conferences, in the mid 60's, the Orthodox Church, in the last twenty-five years, entered into official theological dialogues with several churches and denominations. All these dialogues began with clear intention to create better mutual understanding between the churches, gradually to remove past condemnations and achieve visible unity in one faith and in full sacramental communion.

The Third Pan-Orthodox Preconciliar Conference of 1986, proceeded to a thorough evaluation of these dialogues and in this respect unequivocally declared that the bilaterals were undertaken for both theological and pastoral reasons, with the firm conviction that by entering into theological dialogue with other churches and denominations, the Orthodox Church was bearing witness to her centuries-old tradition, thus paving the way toward unity.

Indeed in the introductory paragraph of the document on the bilaterals, this Preconciliar Conference articulated in the clearest possible way the reasons which prompted the Orthodox Church to embark in theological discussions with the non-Orthodox churches and denominations. "The Orthodox Church," the document said, "being the One, Holy, Catholic and Apostolic Church, is fully conscious of her responsibility with respect to the unity of world Christendom. She recognizes the real existence of all Christian Churches and Confessions. At the same time, she believes that her relations with these Churches and Confessions must be based upon the clarification, as quickly and objectively as possible, of the ecclesiological question and, particularly, of issues concerning their teaching about sacraments, grace, priesthood and apostolic succession. The bilateral theological dialogues currently being conducted by the Orthodox Church, are precisely the authoritative expression of this very consciousness of Orthodoxy."[1]

Presently the Orthodox Church is in theological conversations with the Oriental Orthodox Churches, the Anglican Communion, the Roman Catholic Church, the Lutheran World Federation (representing the Lutheran Communion), and the World Alliance of Reformed Churches (representing denominations of Calvinist/Presbyterian/Congregational background) while she completed a first round of discussions with the Old Catholic Church and is about to inaugurate a theological dialogue with the World Methodist Council.

These dialogues are conducted with varying degrees of success, according to the circumstances and to their historical context. They express however the determination of our Church to facilitate a better understanding between Churches and Denominations and prepare the way towards Christian unity.

In brief, the present state of these dialogues is as follows:

THE ORTHODOX/ORIENTAL ORTHODOX DIALOGUE

Although Orthodox and Oriental Orthodox Churches belong to the same roots and have many things in common, paradoxically this is one of the most recent dialogues. The Joint Orthodox and Oriental Orthodox Theological Commission

---

[1]*Episkepsis*, No. 369, 15 December 1986, p. 9.

had its first official meeting only in December 1985, in Chambésy, Geneva, during which delegates agreed upon the methodology and the agenda of the dialogue. Quite naturally, Christology and ecclesiology were chosen as the main objectives of this dialogue. The second plenary of this Commission met June 20-24, 1989 at Amba Bishoy Monastery in Egypt. It elaborated a common text on the christological dogma and dealt with pastoral issues the Churches are facing today, particularly in the Middle East region. The third plenary of the Commission met again in Chambésy, from September 23 to 28, 1990, and reviewed two reports on theological and pastoral concerns. On the basis of the Amba Bishoy document, the Chambésy plenary unanimously condemned the Eutychian and Nestorian heresies, and declared that both Church traditions "have always loyally maintained the same authentic Orthodox christological faith and the unbroken continuity of the Apostolic Tradition" though they may have used christological terms in different ways. They further stated that "this common faith and continuous loyalty to the Apostolic Tradition, should be the basis of unity and communion between Orthodox and Oriental Orthodox." Consequently they recommended to their respective churches, the lifting of the mutual condemnations and the anathemas pronounced in the context of the Fourth Ecumenical Council of Chalcedon.

In connection with the pastoral dimension of the Orthodox-Oriental Orthodox relationships, the Joint Commission dealt extensively with issues such as mixed marriages, the revision of catechetical books and curricula, the dangers arising from the contemporary secularism, the proliferation of sects, Uniatism, the practice of many Protestant churches of ordaining women, and the evolution of the Ecumenical Movement today from an Orthodox perspective.

The consensus achieved in this dialogue is remarkable indeed. It should be noted, however, that in reaching rapidly a theological convergence on the christological doctrine, the Joint Commission was greatly helped by the findings of the conversations which theologians from the two traditions had during their informal meetings in Aarhus (1964), Bristol (1967), Geneva (1970) and Addis Ababa (1971), made possible through the good offices of Faith and Order.*

THE ORTHODOX/ANGLICAN DIALOGUE

Discussions with Anglicans started already in the 19th century. And they were revived in the mid 60's. After some years of stagnation, however, the International Commission of the Anglican/Orthodox Theological Dialogue started a second round of conversations in 1989 in Finland, under new leadership.

Scripture, Tradition and Councils, ecclesiology, epiclesis, faith and worship, communion of saints, ordination of women, image, symbol and language in relation to the Holy Trinity, the Holy Trinity as Communion, and the Filioque clause were among the subjects dealt with by this Joint Commission. It is interesting to note that at its Finland meeting the Commission recommended that Anglicans consider dropping the Filioque clause in future liturgical revisions. This was an encouraging development. Indeed the resolution of the Filioque controversy, which has for many centuries affected East-West relationships, is of utmost importance and, as the last Lambeth Conference remarked (1988), if the Provinces of the Anglican Communion were to restore the Nicene creed to its original form, there is no doubt that a major difficulty in Anglican-Orthodox relations would have been removed.

Presently, conversations concentrate on the doctrine of the

*Editor's note: The Faith and Order Commission of the World Council of Churches

Person of Jesus Christ, his relationship to the Holy Spirit, to creation and humanity, and to the Church.

THE ORTHODOX/ROMAN CATHOLIC DIALOGUE

This dialogue was inaugurated in 1980 in Patmos/Rhodos. Among the major achievements of this dialogue was the adoption of joint documents on "The Mystery of the Church and the Eucharist in the light of the Mystery of the Holy Trinity," on "Faith, Sacraments and the Unity of the Church" and on "The Sacrament of ordination in the sacramental structure of the Church." This particular text contains chapters about "Christ and the Holy Spirit," "Priesthood in the divine economy of Salvation," "The ministry of the Bishop, the Presbyter and the Deacon" and "The Apostolic Succession."

Because of the resurgence of the Uniate problem however, the Joint Dialogue Commission in its Valamo plenary (1988) was obliged to deal extensively with this particular issue. Consequently it nominated a special Working Group to go more deeply into this matter, which seriously affects Orthodox-Roman Catholic relationships. The Munich (Freising) plenary (6-15 June 1990) was supposed to elaborate a test on "The theological and canonical consequences of the Sacramental Structure of the Church – The reciprocal relationships between authority and canonical conciliarity in the Church." However, because of developments in Eastern Europe related to Uniatism and the deterioration of the situation in Ukraine, Transylvania, Poland and Czechoslovakia, the whole meeting was dedicated to the study of the origins, the existence and the development of the Uniate Churches.

In a public statement, the Joint International Commission recognized that "Uniatism is an urgent problem, to be treated with priority over all other subjects," that as a method unity, is in opposition to the common Tradition of the two churches, and that wherever it was employed as a method, Uniatism failed to achieve its goal of bringing the churches closer together. On the contrary, it provoked new divisions. The Munich plenary emphasized that "dialogue, which is the most suitable way to work for unity, is also the most appropriate form to confront problems, particularly that of Uniatism," and pleaded for the continuation of the Orthodox/Roman Catholic dialogue, since this obstacle of Uniatism 'has in fact to be overcome, if we wish to continue our progress towards unity."

After a suspension of its work for about two years, the Joint Commission is due to meet in Lebanon next June to deal again exclusively with the issue of Uniatism.

The Orthodox/Lutheran Dialogue

The work of the Orthodox-Lutheran joint Commission, was inaugurated in 1981. After some exploratory meetings in order to fix its thematic structure and the methodology to be followed, this Commission was able to produce a first joint text during its Allentown, PA USA, meeting (23-30 May 1985) on the "Divine Revelation," a text which in a way determined the content of the discussion which followed. Thus the Crete meeting of the joint Commission (28 May-2 June 1987), dealt with "Scripture and Tradition," while the Bad Segeberg encounter (1-9 September 1989), produced an agreed statement on "The Canon and the Inspiration of the Holy Scripture."

In this way the exploratory contacts between Orthodox and Lutherans which started already in the 16th century have in our days taken a concrete form, helping the two partners get to know each other better and find at least a common theological vocabulary.

THE ORTHODOX/REFORMED DIALOGUE

The official dialogue between the Orthodox Church and the Churches of the Reformation (represented by the World Alliance of Reformed Churches), was inaugurated at Leuenberg (near Basel) on March 1988. During this meeting participants on the one hand exchanged views about the historical past of the two Churches, and on the other had a first theological discussion about the Nicene-Constantinopolitan Creed, particularly its relevance and interpretation today.

The second Orthodox-Reformed meeting took place in Minsk (Byelorussia) from October 2 to 5, 1990. During the four-day dialogue, the delegates heard presentations and responses on two subjects: "The Biblical and Patristic doctrine on the Trinity" and "The Trinity in the worship of the Church." The speakers were commissioned to expound and clarify the background to the Nicene-Constantinopolitan Creed and to affirm the fundamental agreement of the Orthodox and the Reformed on the Holy Trinity. It was emphasized that, while both traditions subscribe to this Creed and to its trinitarian emphasis, "the reality of the faith in the Trinity is more important than specific theological terminology." It was also stated that it is incumbent upon both traditions to "live and communicate the trinitarian faith today in liturgy, prayers and hymns, in the expression of love and joy in everyday life, in respect for the integrity of creation, and in out critical affirmation of human reason and science, as gifts of God the Creator." A working paper, which outlines specific details about the doctrine agreed upon, was discussed and difference of interpretation were noted.

THE ORTHODOX/METHODIST DIALOGUE

This is still in an exploratory stage. A first planning committee met in July 1992 in Oxford aiming at an initial presentation of each side, in terms of its historical and theological self-understanding and ecclesiology. This committee will meet next July in Constantinople focusing on the "Proclamation of the Gospel" and "The Unity of the Church" (the future of the dialogue might be jeopardized, after the US Methodists' decision to create a Bishopric in Moscow and start missionary work in Russia).

The Orthodox/Old Catholic Dialogue

This is one of the oldest bilateral dialogues of our Church, which started in the 19th century after the first Vatican Council. The dialogue took on an official character in 1965 after the decision of the Third Pan-Orthodox Conference at Rhodes (1964). A variety of theological issues such as the Doctrine of God, Christology, Mariology, the Church and her nature, authority, infallibility, Scripture and Tradition, Apostolic succession, Ecumenical Councils, have been debated and agreed upon in seven plenary meetings of the Mixed Orthodox/Old Catholic Theological Commission. The last meeting of the mixed Commission was held in Kavala, Greece, between 12 and 19 October 1987. Subjects examined during this meeting were on the Sacraments of Penance, of Holy Unction, of Priesthood and of marriage, on eschatology and on ecclesial communion.

The overall results of the Orthodox/Old Catholic discussion were communicated to the Ecumenical Patriarch and to the Archbishop of Utrecht, according to established procedures, in order to declare officially the conclusion of this dialogue.

Needless to say, the ending of the Orthodox/Old Catholic conversations does not automatically mean that sacramental unity between the two Churches can be restored. On the one hand, one has to see how the common theological understanding contained in the agreed statements is going to be incorporated in the official teaching of the two churches and expressed in worship and catechism. On the other hand, one has to wait for an Old Catholic reaction to the Orthodox warning that Sacramental Communion of the Old Catholics with Anglicans, Lutherans and other Protestant Confessions constitutes an impediment for the establishment of full communion between the two churches. Another matter further complicating the anticipated union is the very recent practice of the Old Catholic Church to ordain women to priesthood. The green light given lately to dioceses by the Old Catholic International Congress (Geneva, August 1990) to ordain women at their discussion certainly will not facilitate the relationships.

* * * * *

It is worth noting that these dialogues, by focusing on controversial doctrinal issues which have divided the Churches for centuries, were able to reach remarkable theological agreements and convergencies. By means of careful biblical, historical and theological studies, they managed to restate fundamental convictions of the Christian faith. And although it has not been possible so far to overcome all dividing issues between Christian traditions, the process of bilateral dialogues has, indeed, accelerated the move towards the manifestation of the unity of the Church.

Among the issues debated in most of these bilateral dialogues, we note that ecclesiology occupies a central place. This was a deliberate choice, I believe. As the second Christian millennium draws to a close and we all try to deal with enormously difficult questions about the nature of human community within an increasingly interdependent, yet deeply divided world, questions about the meaning of tradition, the extent of pluralism and the nature of theological conceptuality are raised very often. Faced with these realities, therefore, how must Christians understand the Church's nature, life and witness? What might it mean for the Church to be a sacrament, an instrument of humanity's intimacy with God? Because of these fundamental questions, the bilaterals rightly considered that the delving into the realm of ecclesiology, and formulating a common understanding about the meaning of our belief in the One, Holy, Catholic and Apostolic Church as expressed in the Creed, were the starting points of any further meaningful debate on other doctrinal issues.

In the above effort to define the nature of the Church, we see that almost all bilateral dialogues (and this is relevant also with regard to the bilaterals of the Roman Catholic Church with Protestant denominations or to the Inter-protestant dialogue), place the concept of *koinonia* at the very center of the debate, emphasizing the Trinitarian basis of *koinonia*, considered as participation in the life of God, through Jesus Christ, by the power of the Holy Spirit. At the same time the bilaterals emphasize the four credal marks of the Church: Oneness, Holiness, Catholicity, Apostolicity. And it is interesting to note that, whereas on the question of Christian unity the ecumenical movement emphasizes usually the need for synchronic unity ("unity here and now"), the bilaterals stress the importance of diachronic unity, a unity stretching back to the apostles and forward towards the fulfillment of the Kingdom of God.

* * * * *

The natural question which could be rightly raised by the Orthodox believer or by our theological students ready to start their pastoral ministry in the local level is whether the agreements reached in these dialogues can be meaningful for the people of God or relevant in the context of the day to day life and witness of a parish. This is a quite legitimate question, which should be taken seriously into consideration by those involved in dialogues.

The late Dr. Visser't Hooft once remarked that "There is a very real danger in the bilateral dialogues of becoming esoteric, for they are speaking in a language and formulas which are really understood by those who are participating and not by the average Church members."[2]

Indeed a rational and academic dialogue, based on positions, texts and arguments, a dialogue which overlooks, or even ignores, the pastoral problems of the Churches in a given context, is condemned to remain a theoretical exercise with little impact in the effort to restore Christian unity and with no influence at all on the life of our believers.

It should be admitted by all that the Churches' common journey today in the path leading to the same eucharistic table does not only affect questions of doctrine but also joint action, which has become imperative in recent years. This is why I think that pastoral, social and ethical problems can no longer be excluded from the bilateral dialogues, but they should be given higher priority. Because analogous to the connection between doctrine and worship is the inseparable connection between orthodoxia and orthopraxia, an orthopraxia which makes ethics, not less than dogmatics, an indispensable element of any interchurch dialogue. Church doctrine, spirituality and action are so intimately interrelated that they are all integral parts of today's ecumenical dialogue.

---

[2] W. A. Visser't Hooft, "The Place of Bilateral conversation in the Ecumenical Movement," in *Études Théologiques* 5, Les Dialogues oecuméniques hier et aujourd'hui, Chambésy 1986, p. 139.

Orthodoxy and Ecumenism:
Critical Ecclesiastical Reflections

Rev. Milton B. Efthimiou

Prologue

Many will remember the 20th century as the "Century of Ecumenism." Several ecumenists, theologians, canonists, and just plain religious folk, both pro-ecumenism and contra-ecumenism, have expressed their sentiments throughout the recent past. We hear some say that the last 50 years have been the richest in Christian history. Others say that we are in "stagnation if not resignation" (Konrad Raiser, the new General Secretary of the World Council of Churches). What does all this mean for the Orthodox? What kind of criteria can we use to evaluate the present status of things? Listen to what one writer says:

> For Christians cannot be distinguished from the rest of the human race by country or language or customs . . . Yet, they live in their own countries, but obey as aliens . . . Every foreign land is their fatherland, and yet for them every fatherland is a foreign land . . . They busy themselves on earth, but their citizenship is in heaven . . . ! To put it simply: What the soul is in the body, Christians are in the world. The soul is dispensed through all the members of the body, and Christians are scattered through all the cities of the world . . . the soul dwells in the body, but does not belong to the

body, and Christians dwell in the world, but do not belong to the world.

Do you know where this quote is from? Second Century *Epistle to Diognetos*. For me, this is the criterion . . .! Perennial truth that guide us whether it is 1st century or 20th. Allow me to come down to the 20th century.

The decision of the Standing Conference of Canonical Bishops in the Americas (SCOBA) on October 14, 1991, to suspend its participation in the National Council of Churches of Christ, and subsequently to suspend dialogue with the Anglicans was an unprecedented action of great importance.* Especially significant is the provisional presumption of membership in the NCCC until 1994 when the action will again be reviewed by SCOBA.

The fact that the hierarchs of SCOBA unanimously chose to concur with the earlier decision of Archbishop Iakovos, who is chairman of SCOBA, and the Synod of Bishops of the Greek Orthodox Archdiocese on June 6, 1991 to suspend participation in the NCCC and with the Anglicans, indicates that all the jurisdictions of SCOBA have serious concerns about the direction of concilliar ecumenism, especially now that these concerns have extended to the Roman Catholic Church and the whole subject of "Uniatism," or Eastern Churches in Communion with Rome, which are a constant reminder of the painful experience of the whole specter of "proselytism" by western missionaries in Orthodox Eastern Europe and the Orthodox Middle East during long periods of politico-cultural weakness, when most of the Orthodox peoples were under Islamic or Western subjugation. The above challenges involving a variety of issues, some of which we will discuss further

---

*Editor's note: This was SCOBA's reaction to the application of the Metropolitan Community Church to join the NCCC. The suspension with the Anglican Church is discussed later in this paper.

on, have been at the forefront on all of our dialogues here in the US, and are the basis of motivation of the Ecumenical Office of the Archdiocese, which also serves as the Ecumenical Office, for the time being, of SCOBA.

But before we delve into the subject of Orthodoxy and its relation to other Church bodies or denominations, we need to affirm our commitment to the process of Christian reconciliation. We need to affirm that Christian disunion is a scandal, and contrary to what we pray for in the Eucharist Sunday after Sunday: "Let us pray to the Lord for the peace of the world, the stability of the Holy Churches of God and for the union of all!"

Guided by Scripture and Tradition, we affirm our obligation to seek to overcome misunderstandings and doctrinal differences which have contributed to the disunity of Christians. We also affirm our responsibilities to join with other Christians of good will in appropriate councils, forums and consultations which seek to overcome misunderstanding, to heal divisions and to foster unity in the Faith of the Apostles of Christ.

The Ecumenical Patriarchate has consistently provided us with inspiration and wisdom in these efforts for reconciliation, as well as in the challenge of dialogue with other Christians. Most recently, His All Holiness Patriarch Bartholomew reminded us of the special responsibility which Orthodoxy has today. "In Orthodoxy, we can find not only the correct faith in the true God, but also the correct perception of the human person as the image of God, of the world, and of creation."

"Ecumenism": A Definition

We have been using this term, "ecumenism," and I am afraid that some of us do not understand the term. I raise this question because I had the impression from my experiences in the various dialogues which I either cöordinate or chair, that the term gives way to an easy generalization. As is usually the case with almost all terms that end in "-ism," "ecumenism" may indicate a kind of contemporary ideology, i.e. a kind of *Weltanschauung* as the Germans would say, which interprets world reality and proceeds to solve problems in definitive ways and consistent action. An ideology understood in this way, risks falling into the temptation of exclusiveness and absolutism, especially in socio-political struggles and, for our intents and purposes, theological debates. "Ecumenism" in this sense cannot be applied in the case of the church or the Ecumenical Office of the Archdiocese because we are not called upon to evaluate any ideologies in praxis or competition against other ideologies of a similar kind. When churches convert their faith into action, we are entirely dependent on the collaboration between the transcending grace of God and all endeavors that are human, so that with all our weaknesses and failures, we act in concert. The late Dr. Nikos Nissiotis, one of the great ecumenists of the 20th century, Professor of Theology at the University of Athens, once said that the term "ecumenism" denotes the decision, the existence, and the action of the churches linked together in one organization in collaboration of service to the world. By extension of this definition by Nissiotis, the term also expresses the "diakonia" of churches that think and act together, regardless of their confessional differences, on the basis of Christian faith. This faith unifies those churches in a new fellowship, through a variety of expressions, through different forms, but of the one and same movement. Historically, ecumenism came from movements entirely independent from each other at the beginning of the ecumenical era: From World Christian Youth and student organizations, from missionary societies, from conferences of dogmatic and moral theologians, from Christian social thinkers and activists, and others. All of these movements have three things in common: First, the inter-church composition of their membership; second, their devotion to the mandate of the one Christian faith to share together in one church fellowship; and third, the belief that Christian thinking and acting together become more capable of a better and fuller ministry to the Gospel. These three things were brought together by basically one man in 1955. The story of this one man was cited at Canberra, Australia, by Philip Potter who at the time was secretary of the Youth Department of the World Council of Churches. He eventually became one of the great General Secretaries of the WCC. Mr. Potter described this man, new on the scene, as follows:

> He came to Geneva in 1955 as the first representative of the Ecumenical Patriarchate and Patriarch Athenagoras. A warm friendship grew between us. He was always a welcome guest in our house, even when he used to destroy us in a new game of words called "Scramble." He had mastered the English of Boston to give us a hard time! But what he did remained forever that basis of the ecumenical movement.

Of course, that man was no one other than Iakovos Coucouzis, who went on to become not only one of the greatest acknowledged ecumenists of our time, but Archbishop of the Americas. Now, in order to understand our topic for today, Orthodoxy in terms of ecumenism and inter-church relations, and the future of this relationship, in answer to those who outright condemn the ecumenical movement, you have to understand what happened back then, so let me continue. As Bishop of Melitis, Iakovos came to Geneva with the implicit knowledge of the initiative which had been taken in 1920 by Ecumenical Patriarchate in proposing a League (Koinonia) of Churches as a counterpart to the efforts of a League of Nations. He saw as his task interpreting the work of the council to all the Orthodox Churches around the world. He developed the three points mentioned above to churches in the Mediterranean, the Orthodox churches in Eastern Europe, and pioneered the way for their becoming members of the council in the early 1960s. When he left Geneva in 1959 to be Archbishop in the Americas, he continued the same role, and was soon elected president of the WCC. During those years, he used his influence for the unity of the Church for its witness into a deeply divided and broken world. It is this advocacy that continues to motivate the Archbishop in conformance to the prayer of our Lord that we all may be one, even as He and the Father shared a co-inherent life, so that by sharing this life with Him and the Father and with each other, the world may believe.

Professor Günter Gassman, the head of Faith and Order in Geneva and one of the few remaining ecumenists from the early days, reminded me recently that one of the driving forces in the movement in the early days that Iakovos spearheaded was fellowship in prayer. This later was epitomized in the Week of Prayer for Christian Unity, celebrated throughout the world in all Churches the month of January. Fr. George Tsetsis shared this with me recently. He calls it the "Iakovian legacy" for cultivating respect and trust among the ecumenical partners in dialog which led into a relationship of mutual accountability to one another in Christ's Name at all times. However differently all this has been appropriated and expressed during the years, there can be no doubt that in the quest for reconciliation, there have been of late some serious tendencies which threaten this mutual accountability. I know it saddens many of the old guard. Among these we would note: the tendency among some to diminish the significance of the trinitarian understanding of God, as we saw at the last WCC meeting in Canberra, Australia; to disregard classical Christian teachings on moral and ethical issues, such as the recognition of homosexuality as a basis for acceptance in the NCCC; the recognition of woman's ordination, including gays' and lesbians' ordination, a key factor in our estrangement with the Anglican Church, as witnessed at the recent upheaval of the Anglican world-wide Conference in Capetown, S. Africa; and the tendency to diminish the Christian role of acceptable missionary imperatives of the Gospel, as witnessed by the Latin Church's proselytism in Orthodox lands.

These tendencies led us at times to seriously question whether there is always sufficient "common ground" between Orthodoxy and certain other Christians to continue a theological dialogue which has as its ultimate goal the visible unity of Christians rooted in the common understanding of the Apostolic Faith. Without, therefore, diminishing our commitment to Christian reconciliation, as we learned it in the process developed by giants like Iakovos, Potter, Nissiotis, Blake, Hooft, Espy and others, our task is to go back to our fundamentals of theology and which councils, forums and consultations are appropriate for our participation. Recently, the Catholic/Orthodox Metropolitan Dialogue, of which I am co-chairman, has been put in suspension because a common marriage document for use by priests in both churches as a brochure to prospective married couples for counseling has bogged down on some theological and canonical questions surrounding issues of the Sacrament itself, the bringing up of children, the question of Communion in both Churches, etc. In determining the proper forum for these discussions, the Orthodox churches will again be marking a new phase in ecumenical relations, because in affirming that Orthodoxy represents the one unbroken Church of the Triune God, the other churches must keep before them the primacy and urgency of the issues of unity. Orthodox scholars have already begun to do this. In Brazil, last summer, at the "Earth Summit," scientists and technologists are now raising with the Orthodox profound questions about Creation and about human responsibility on the use of nature and the resources of the earth. Events have pushed Roman Catholicism and Protestantism to recover a Theology of Creation, and as a result, prompted the late great Patriarch Dimitrios I, to issue a stunning document called "Orthodoxy and Ecological Crisis" which forced one and all to rethink and recover a Theology of Creation which grows out of our faith in the Triune God Who is Creator, Redeemer, Sustainer and Perfector of life and creation. Orthodoxy and its theology will, I believe, be a major player in the thinking of this vital issue in a world which is riddled with the threats to survival and yet has the immense possibilities of creating a more just and sustainable society. This summer this topic will be discussed at length at Santiago de Compostela, Spain, at the Fifth World Conference on Faith and Order of the World Council of Churches.

Which leads us now to do something very painful: A self evaluation of Orthodoxy, a critique if you will, based on what has already taken place and which we summarized above. Let us call this critique:

ORTHODOXY TODAY – BEYOND ECUMENISM

In 1994 Orthodoxy will celebrate the Bicentennial of the first permanent Russian Orthodox Community in Alaska. In

1768, the First Greek Orthodox colonists on what is now U.S. territory came to St. Augustine, Florida. And yet, despite our many years in North America, despite our great strides in Ecumenism, the collective contribution of the Orthodox Churches to the American ethos and culture has been negligible.

Why? At this point, we can turn our eyes to those whom we consistently claim to be our examples and teachers, our Holy Fathers of the Church, and look for a moment into their deep understanding of living in the present. We saw this somewhat with Diognetos' Epistle in the beginning of this talk.

Most certainly, the Fathers were not less intellectual than us. Yet, there is one decisive difference between them and modern day ecumenists and theologians: the eternal salvation of man. Words and ideas were from them directly related not simply to Truth and Error, but to the Truth that "saves" and to the Error that brings with it death and damnation. And it is their total constant, truly "existential" preoccupation with, and their total commitment to salvation of real people, that make every line they wrote so vital and so precisely pastoral.

Intellectual as it is, their theology is always addressed not to "intellectuals," but to the whole church, in the firm belief that everyone in the Church has received the spirit of Truth, and this is always translated to the "practical," the pastoral needs of every individual rooted in their theological implications.

Now, what does all this mean . . . now that we are on the threshold of the 21st century . . . now that the year A.D. 2000 is fast approaching! We have a solid past to guide us, because religion has shaped American Culture from the earliest settlements, right here in Boston, in Virginia, etc., from the early immigrants who established vibrant ethnic religious communities here. But to use the word of a priest who works at the

"Ethics and Public Policy Center" in Washington, D.C., "all is not right in the American public square." I like that term. I used it in a report to the Archdiocesan Council recently that received some notoriety when I tried to show that basically the Churches in America, all part of the Ecumenical Movement, have for the most part failed in terms of the urgency for thinking about the challenge to discard everything that is traditional, cultured, ethnic as stereotypes, so that with our sense of continuity and respect for the *status quo* being blurred and confused, with what has now been true under fire and what has been once accepted now under fire and what has been once accepted now considered obsolete, we have backed ourselves into a political quagmire, long before the protestant attempts to liberalize theology or sexual morality. And so, there is today a vacuum in that "public square," words also used in a recent best selling book by Richard Neuhaus, "The Naked Public Square."

Now, why are we absent from this so-called "public square?" If our theology is true and on target, why has Orthodoxy abandoned its traditional role of evangelizing! And yet, when it's done by everyone else, we complain or get threatened!

Allow me to cite but one statistic: the Religion of Islam. The *New York Times* ran a series on Muslims last week and showed how the 4 million Muslims are growing by leaps and bounds in 1,100 parishes in the U.S., 80% of which were built in the last 12 years. Notice: *in the last 12 years!* Should we be concerned or not? Should we be concerned that our church, the keeper of sacred traditions common to all faiths and denominations, is absent from a milieu in which every Orthodox person is immersed today?

Should we be concerned that Orthodox Christianity has even abandoned traditional meanings to once sacrosanct terms: "Salvation" now means self-fulfillment; "Faith" means security;

"Sin" means a personal problem of adjustment, etc., and when others look at us, what do they see? A church fragmented along jurisdictional/ethnic lines, some of whom think of us as an exotic Catholic community, confusing the ancient Orthodox churches with Eastern or Byzantine Rite Catholic churches; still others, mostly the Protestants belonging to the NCCC thinking of us as a "Protestant" equivalent to something like non-Roman Catholic, ergo, a "denomination" like others; and still others, when told we are "Orthodox," ask, "What Jewish branch do you belong to?"

Enter the Orthodox in a technological society.

Some of you may, by now, feel offended by what I have said. But can we all at least agree that in the U.S., as elsewhere, we have today an "identity" crisis? And if so, must we not put the blame at the doorstep of the Orthodox Churches themselves? Does it not become ever more painful when we realize that at one time the Byzantine milieu of World Christendom was centered at the Ecumenical Patriarchate of which Orthodox Churches everywhere – Greece, Finland, Russia, Serbia, Romania – anywhere in the world, these were and are the collective heirs of that whole milieu and civilization? In the countries mentioned, and so many others which I didn't mention? Doesn't it mean anything that what happened for Orthodox Christians world-wide, who retained Byzantium's majesty tenaciously perpetuating the rich social, political and cultural heritage, *even when their societies crumbled*, has not happened in America?

I need not remind us that Byzantium was not just a Greek phenomenon; it was multinational and lasted more than a millennium. It was a "Federation" of diverse peoples and cultures united in one imperial society. The "pluralism" of the U.S. mirrors this "Federation" or "Commonwealth" of different peoples so well, and, as a result, America can learn from the Byzantine experience. But only if we make it happen, just as in Byzantium "imperium" and "sacerdotum" between Church and State created a model, which, admittedly didn't always work, for cöoperation on contemporary social and religious issues for people who made a policy in the "public arena" (I might cite here the brilliant study of Fr. Constantelos, "Byzantine Philanthropy and Social Welfare," where we see examples of both Church and State caring for the sick, elderly, homeless, etc.). These Byzantines prefigured contemporary American values of social compassion and concerns, like pornography, ecology, healthcare, etc., that politicians in Congress down to President Clinton often talk about.

Conclusion

In the prologue, an *"anaskopisis,"* a review of history, which began with the decision to suspend with the NCCC and working backwards, was our way of coming to the point here of suggesting that the Orthodox Community must find ways and means of engaging an American society and culture in dialogue. We will henceforth be navigating through uncharted waters, so we must be careful, because this implies risk – a dialogue implies the possibility of being changed by the other. Byzantine civilization, however romantic the Orthodox might remember it, cannot be simply "transplanted" to America. Nor is Washington going to become Byzantium on the Potomac, as someone has said. But if we are going to be in dialogue with the Roman Catholics, Protestants, Anglicans, Copts, Jacobites, etc. we must do two things:

First, because we are living on the threshold of the 21st century and the year A.D. 2000 is fast approaching, the urgency for thinking in terms of tomorrow's context of what constitutes our Byzantine legacy must motivate us to challenge and sometimes even discard various stereotypes, without blurring our sense of continuing and respect for a meaningful past. To me "Orthodoxy and Ecumenism," our topic, rises and falls on this very issue, mainly because we are living in the most exciting, yet most threatening era in which to theologize. "Theologizing" is, as someone recently stated in one of our dialogues, the rigorous and daily exercise of relating the word of God to the human world. This means, for all of us, that the context of our theologizing must be global. Where we, the Orthodox are often guilty, is that we limit our "theologizing" to parochialism. Parochial theologizing is antiquated, if not very destructive in our day. The ecumenical movement has taught us that we have come from an age of disputes to one of dialogue, from divergence to convergence, from polemics to irenics, as much as possible. The world has created an environment which theology can no longer ignore. Theology must recapture that legacy during Byzantine times . . . , it can no longer be an irrelevant exercise in this age of technology and space, with irrelevant theologians who are either steeped in political agendas, marginalizing their Churches from the "public arena" that essentially determines public policy, to the other extreme, where theologians simply rehash yesterday's battles and neglect the Eternal Contemporary, the Lord of the Cosmos and of universal history. What I am suggesting is that we must articulate this eschatological dimension within our churches as well as within our cities.

Second, we must interpret that tradition to Americans faithful to Christ's admonition to witness to all nations enabling everyone to do what we have said, to help him/her understand and hear the true teaching of the Church. This metamorphosis must take place first and foremost in our own

Parishes. We must begin, therefore, with what Patristic Theology performed in its time: an exorcism of culture, a liberating reconstruction of symbols, words, the theological language itself, not to make our theology more "acceptable" to the modern man in the "public square," but, on the contrary, to make him/her aware of the ultimately serious and eschatological demands of his/her faith.

Only theology can accomplish this, and this is why it is so badly needed today. But it will only succeed when it becomes again "pastoral," i.e. identified with the Church and her life, attentive to the real needs of man, in humility and with language that is comprehensible and meaningful.

It is this synthesis of idealism and realism, of vision and faith, of religion and justice, all part of our heritage that just might speak forcefully to the role of Orthodoxy in the contemporary world for, to say that Jesus Christ is our hope and our destiny, is to say that Jesus Christ is our hope and our destiny, is to say that Christianity is eschatology, which means that the essence of the Christian faith is hope, for all peoples, whether in Russia, Middle East, Bosnia, Serbia, U.S.A., in hope that looks to the future and moves forward, transforming and revolutionizing the present.

A Reformed View of
the Santiago Conference

Antoinette C. Wire

After a major event such as the Fifth World Conference on Faith and Order in Spain this August, the challenge is not simply to tell what happened but to consider its significance for us as American Christians. I can speak only tentatively as a person new to Faith and Order work and as a delegate of a specific denomination, the Presbyterian Church (U.S.A.). But I consider it important that we review what it means that for that the first time official world-wide delegates of Orthodox, Roman Catholic and Protestant churches came together to work toward reclaiming the faith that unites all churches.

A recent diagnosis of our Presbyterian church is that we will thrive only if we learn to think theologically. This month two articles in the U.S. Presbyterian-related press written from opposite ends of the theological spectrum made the same point that we must "recover our theological vision," find "the will of God," and "urgently transmit a true theological . . . voice." Though they hardly faced the shocking nature of their diagnosis that our faith is without God, we recognize truth in their challenge to seek God. If it is our purpose, the question about the Santiago conference is whether a theological vision was presented there that can center us again in unity with our sister churches and can at the same time give us a dynamic contemporary language for speaking about God.

In fact a theological vision was presented which we must seriously consider, at the same as we ask whether it is adequate to the God we know in Christ. The years of work which developed this theology are attested in the recent Faith and Order document, *Confessing the One Faith*, which explicates the Nicene-Constantinopolitan Creed. But *Confessing the One Faith* is a tightly-packed doctrinal study and in its present form does not evoke the historical struggle that might bring this creed to life. Fortunately, the conference delegates were not put to debating its articles but received instead an article called "Koinonia in Faith, Life and Witness" which became a stimulus to group discussion resulting in the conference reports that are now available with this report as Fifth World Conference on Faith and Order (Faith and Order paper #164).

The starting point for this study was the Greek term "koinonia" – meaning communion, sharing, partnership, or solidarity. As interpreted in addresses to the conference by the Lutheran Wolfhart Pannenberg, the Orthodox John Zizioulas, and the Roman Catholic Jean-Marie Tillard, God represents for us true communion, being three distinct persons in one nature. The universe in its great diversity comes from the God the Creator who wills the solidarity of all that is. But the humans threaten their own destruction and that of the created world, God incarnate in Christ joins the victims in their life and death, and God the Spirit draws them through Christ's rising into living participation in the divine communion.

The power if this vision of God for today is that it depicts the Trinity of the common Creed as a non-hierarchical communion that is the source of all creation, a communion that reaches out to incorporate the prodigal human being in an active, and potentially cosmic, common life. When the visible unity that has always been the goal of the Faith and Order movement is understood to have its foundation in the communion of God's own being, which is both the ground of cosmic solidarity and the source of human restoration to community, then the church need not despair its brokenness but can let all its rich history ferment together into good compost to make a seed-bed for communion in our fractured world.

Yet difficulties with this trinitarian model of divine koinonia were expressed at the Santiago conference that we need to take equally seriously as we seek a clearer vision of God's presence in our time.

When fifty delegates from Reformed Churches of the world gathered in an informal meeting, the objection was expressed that the Lutherans were courting the Orthodox and Catholics so intently that the Bible had all but disappeared behind the Nicene Creed. Pannenberg had gone so far as to say that because the Nicene-Constantinopolitan Creed was the only early creed intended to provide a summary of the faith for the whole church, each new confession has to be tested by it and the complete witness of Scripture is present in it by implication. Such narrowing of the authoritative base of the Christian faith to a single creed in a single context was unacceptable to many delegates who claimed a far broader biblical foundation of our koinonia. The Roman Catholic Bishop Onaiyekan of Nigeria traced the Abraham story of communion with Jews and Muslims today. Dorothy Lee of the Uniting Church in Australia focused on the way Mary of Bethany in John's Gospel fully embodies communion with Christ, who is both death-suffering and life-giving power. Frances Young, a Methodist Professor from the University of Birmingham, challenged us in Bible studies each morning to take seriously both Paul and his opponents in Galatia as contending witness to the work of God's Spirit in the church.

It was clear in the meticulous biblical study on the term

"koinonia" prepared for the conference by John Reumann of the Evangelical Lutheran Church in America that, when Christians accept the Bible as their common authority, their life in relation to God cannot be comprehended by any single vision or theme. The word "koinonia" does not appear either in the Greek Old Testament or in the gospels. Yet it is an important term in Paul, 1 John and Acts where the Jewish-rooted gospels enter the Hellenistic city. In this impersonal urban world Christians were called into communion or solidarity, living out Jesus' death and rising as His corporate body by giving thanks to God, supporting the needy and receiving each other's leadership. Reumann noted that the inner life of the Trinity is not so much described as koinonia in the biblical texts. The Bible does not so much define God as express communion with God's Spirit and in communion with each other for mission and service. It is this kind of dynamic expression of faith in God, spoken as appropriate in each different context, that makes the Bible such a rich common authority for the church. Perhaps we can envision the triune God more dynamically as the initial and ultimate communion for all if it is not reduced to an official reading of a single normative creed.

The most clearly voiced dissatisfaction with this trinitarian theology at Santiago was expressed by some delegates from Africa, Asia and Latin America. As an Indian delegate put it, we believe in the Father, the Son and the Spirit, but that doesn't get us very far on the issues that divide us. This does not so much deny trinitarian communion but presses beyond it for words to claim solidarity where few are Christians or where Christian cultures have been oppressive. Archbishop Keshishian of Lebanon in this vein of the challenge to live out the unity God gives within local languages and cultures. Yemba Kekumba called the ecumenical movement to open itself to theologies being developed where the church is a growing, mission-oriented minority in a non-Christian culture. Near the end of the conference Gao Ying, the first representative to any Faith and Order conference from China, challenged Faith and Order to develop long-term regional theological consultations with local agendas, and the moderator repeated this proposal in the closing statement of the conference. Clearly many delegates saw the focus on the Nicene creed today as a European theology formulated by European theologians to heal European divisions and not an adequate way to meet the divisions of churches and peoples across the world.

This objection must not be dismissed as the impatience of newcomers with long-term Faith and Order agendas. There are basic issues at stake. In Metropolitan Zizioulas' presentation of the trinitarian koinonia, for example, the diversity in the church made possible by the divine communion was said to include the natural divisions of race, sex and age as well as the social difference of rich and poor, powerful and weak, because all are "needful of one another." But those who find themselves dispossessed rather than privileged by these divisions know that so-called natural divisions are socially constructed, and the social divisions of rich and poor are not mutually beneficial and must be legitimated as appropriate diversities within the communion in Christ. There are substantive reasons for people and culture not in positions of power to be wary of unity on existing terms.

The very organization of Faith and Order work by which theologians in major centers produce the bulk of the work and the scattered churches receive it – or often don't receive it – is being put in question. Melanie May of the Church of the Brethren is now speaking of a new paradigm in which the primary work is local and regional, and the global task becomes to share the fruits of what is produced in each region. If this happens, are we in North America part of the European region because of the origin of some of our people and many of our churches, or would we want to work toward unity independently, perhaps giving special attention to cultural pluralism and economic and gender justice? I would like to press these proposals further by suggesting that Faith and Order reorganize itself into five parallel regional offices, each region of the world making its own proposals about its office location, its staff (there are now five persons in Geneva), and its theological work. Although it is probable that people would favor something like the traditional divisions in Europe, North America, Latin America, Asia/Pacific, Africa and the Middle East, those of us on the West Coast of North America could try to bring off a grouping of the northern hemisphere by oceans: the Pacific, the Indian and its Gulfs, and the Atlantic, to complement Latin America and Africa in the South. Imagine the creative possibilities for us in the American West to work with East Asians toward a Christian theology adequate to the Pacific Basin today! This would be a positive way to receive the theology of God's all-enfolding inner communion as a welcome step toward European church unity and as a challenge to make progress in parallel Christian theologies elsewhere.

Finally there are those who are saying that no concept, even a concept of God, can unite the churches. At the opening worship service in the Cathedral of St. James the local Archbishop Torrella was very frank. He said we can make headway only if we have "an attitude of penance for our part in continuing the divisions among Christians . . . , a spirit of metanoia that allows God to transform our minds and hearts." This alone can open us to God's grace which makes us one. To hear the call to repentance and grace, so familiar from childhood Baptist conferences, in this strange and wonderful cathedral, where the incense censer was swinging across the transept in a great arc from rose window to another in honor of the year of St. James, made me realize that unity is not impossible but is already present if we could only wake up to it. The event of worship – and it was an event – was followed by others in which the Orthodox priests chanted us to heaven and the Spanish Protestant preachers in a Franciscan gothic church gave communion to so many that the bread ran out. Meanwhile each day in opening prayer we sang the simple lines "Tell us, Lord, where did we go astray?" So we learned what the new WCC General Secretary Konrad Raiser put into words at the end, that to find unity we must undergo in our time a conversion to Christ, who is the mystery of our oneness.

If it is worship of God – repentance and praise – that must become our route to unity, it was fitting to be on that pilgrimage in the city of Santiago de Compostela. It is situated in Spain's Northwest corner and was the goal of a great medieval pilgrimage route from Britain, Germany and Italy through France and across Spain to the ends of the earth where the Lord was thought to have sent the Apostle James to preach the Gospel. This summer some of us went early to Spain in order to walk part of the way to Santiago with the modern pilgrims, up every morning before six in the one-room hostels along the route and off on the path with students and priests and brickmasons for another 25 kilometer day. A pilgrimage is never simple, in this case because you see in the Romanesque village churches along the way two kinds of statues of St. James: the intense pilgrim with bare feet and staff, and – by a conflation of symbols with Charlemagne and the Spanish kings – James on a horse brandishing a sword over beheaded Moors. So you pray for repentance again and watch each step to make sure that you are following the right James, talking about this as you accompany each other on the way.

Not so differently, we American Christians are on the way toward unity, alternately wary and weary. But we are learning the eagerness of pilgrims, pressing toward new visions of God on the horizon that unite us with all God's people in God's world.

The Walls Have Fallen:
Building Koinonia in
Faith, Life and Witness

Jeffrey Gros, F.S.C.

In cycling reflectively in the weeks after the World Conference, two random intrusions brought forcefully to mind the paradigm shift that has begun to take place since the 1963 Fourth World Conference:

First, the Jesuit Monthly, *El Mesaje ca*rried an item about the Archbishop of York raising again the question about disestablishing, noting that it was only Protestant and Orthodox churches in Europe, that were still established state churches. Indeed, as late as 1970 James Mitchner could wonder if it would ever be possible to imagine something "ecumenical" in the city of Santiago de Compostela! Ironically, when change came it was the Protestants who rushed to sign the first post-Franco, post-Patronato concordat. Some of us wondered whether it was a good idea when the Orthodox and Protestant leadership selected this city, and the Archbishop-host found it strange that the Protestant worship committee leadership asked for the use of the 1,000 year old cathedral and the odd Botofumeiro ritual and its song for the opening service of the Conference, when the city is filled with much more irenic and contemporary worship forms and music [You may well have read my published observations elsewhere.]

Second, on the first Sunday out on the cycle, at the local cathedral in Bayonne (that historic and once great ecclesiastical capital of the Basque provinces, now divided between Spain and France, is now a sleepy tourist town of no great ecumenical or academic prominence) carried a large section of the message of the Conference in its parish bulletin. In the dominant Church, in these two countries where the Catholic faith and the culture had been so identified for centuries – an anti-enlightenment, anti-Protestant culture at that – the agenda of ecumenical openness, religious liberty and the specific results of faith and order are integral to the religious identity and the pastoral program of the Church leadership. The conversion, so central a spiritual motif of the Conference, is well begun in these Churches.

Indeed, the reception of the ecumenical movement by the Roman Catholic Church is now well established, worldwide in 1965, in Spain in 1973, and reiterated by Cardinal Cassidy at Santiago. The reception of the Roman Catholic Church into the modern ecumenical movement is now well begun, with this first World Conference with official Catholic representation, though the style and worship of the Conference itself still carries the marks of its Protestant origins. In this short comment I will:

1) Review the key issues from the section reports;
2) Focus on some significant factors in the meeting for Roman Catholics;
3) Elaborate on some of the future agenda elements outlined;
4) Note an impression about the spirituality of the Conference;
5) Lift up some hope for the US churches and ecumenical movement;
6) Make some personal comments on the event as an ecumenical marker in our pilgrimage toward full *koinonia*.

It is the thesis of this reporter that this global event signals the end of the Reformation and of Eurocentric Christianity, but that its outline for a united Church will only emerge with careful study, intercultural dialogue and massive conversion to the vision of the unity of the Church for the renewal of human community. Conflict oriented press, ego bruised bureaucrats or distinguished activists should not be taken as the measure of such a monumental gathering empowered by the Spirit of Christ.

1) The message of the Conference is clear in its reiteration of the goal of full, visible unity as central to the ecumenical movement and lifts up the importance of the method of dialogue, cross-cultural, biblical and theological, in the bilaterals, and faith and order in contributing to this goal. It outlines, and the section reports elaborate in some detail, the progress to date and the agenda to come. The Conference was wise not to attempt to produce theological texts or to write theology on the spot, with fine bilateral texts and three background documents of Faith and Order, World Council, as foundation for the section reports and message.

The most precise section reports are II on the Faith dimension, outlining the confessional progress and outstanding issues for further work; and III on *Sacramental Life*, where the "harvesting" theme recurrent in the preparation and planning of the Conference is most evident.

The first section on Koinonia is quite adequate as stating from this most widely diverse group in the ecumenical movement the affirmation of this theme, and the careful distinctions in its biblical understanding, is a central motif for grounding ecclesiology. In this it is an elaboration of the Amsterdam basis of the WCC, and its Toronto (1950) specification; and a gathering up of the bilateral work, and the Nairobi (1975) vision of a Councilor Communion into a common ground.

Finally, the fourth section on Common Witness reiterates the differentiated unity of the ecumenical movement with various aspects: mission, interreligious dialogue, work for Justice, Peace and the Integrity of Creation and evangelism being grounded in the quest for visible unity and growing out of a common commitment to the Gospel of Jesus Christ. It grounds Common Witness in the theological progress toward common confession and common sacramental life. In this Faith and Order does not usurp the other dimensions of the ecumenical movement, nor does it lose its focus of contributing to resolving those theological issues that keep the churches from full communion.*

2) The Third World and women's presences were essential. Tutu's press on the unity agenda, commenting that: "A divided Church is too weak for apartheid" may be the most quotable text for the next decade! Of course, the Protestant dominance leads to certain ironies, like fewer Catholics from Latin America and the Philippines than Protestants, thus di-

---

*Two background papers, not with the maturity of the three Faith and Order (F&O) texts and process, but very helpful, were also made available to the participants. A series of commentaries on the Canberra text on *koinonia* filled out both the importance of that text and its linking with the other elements in the ecumenical movement. A second report from a conference with Justice, Peace and the Integrity of Creation (JPIC) participants, *Costly Unity*, like other F&O / JPIC conferences before Seoul, became a sign and resource for collaboration. While I am not aware of the utilization of any of the language from the F&O preparatory material from the Seoul texts, *Costly Unity* provides a useful witness to collaboration and a hopeful sign of more theological and reflective methods in the JPIC process.

minishing the inclusiveness and diversity . . . As a Roman Catholic, it was pleasing to see the full complement of Orthodox present, even though sometimes with necessary dissent – for whatever motive. This presence was not possible in June when the Orthodox met with the Roman Catholic Church in Lebanon.

We, of course, need to be supersensitive not to further exacerbate the internal polarities among the Byzantine Orthodox. We can only be grateful for the patience and care of ecumenical colleagues like Father Milton and others throughout the world who fight to keep the Orthodox in the ecumenical movement, while avoiding internal divisions among themselves. Indeed, the threat of some Orthodox to reiterate the long dead practice of presenting an Eastern Orthodox separate statement, was carefully and skillfully avoided, the US press – even secular-oriented religious press – notwithstanding. With the ever changing situation in the Middle East and Eastern Europe, these relationships, no matter how vulnerable, will remain extremely important for the long term future.

It was also encouraging to see the full integration of Pentecostal voices from North America into the process. The Pentecostal/Roman Catholic dialogue of almost two decades has begun to pay off in the quality and seriousness of the engagement of theologians from these churches and a relative openness of the leader to allow for, if not yet encourage, such contacts.

3) Focus for future agenda began to become clear and was affirmed by those delegated by their churches to speak for the leadership: In addition to continuation of the collaboration with the mission, interreligious dialogue and Justice, Peace and Integrity units of the World Council, the continued work on the

sacramental, Gospel, culture and confessional issues in the context of an ecclesiology of *koinonia* there were specific recommendations:

I) The authority issue in ecclesiology will be taken up again. While the language used: "structures of mutual accountability," resonates more with the reformed tradition, Catholics will recognize this formulation as *communio hierarchia* (translated by Cardinal Willebrands as "the differentiated character of the Body of Christ"), Anglicans "bonds of communion" etc. What formulation and what theological background and recommended structures for the present and future context will, of course, be the subject of research and dialogue. This will be an important dimension of ecclesiology, no matter how delicate in all of our churches, to give our work on mission, sacraments and confession credibility.

II) We have been called to look again at the hermeneutical question. We find this call also in the evaluations of BEM and the bilateral dialogues coming from our churches. There is a call for the healing of memories and new hermeneutics, ecumenically conceived, of history. Some work has been done in Faith and Order WCC, more in the Reformed/Roman Catholic bilateral and even more – at least conceptually – in Faith and Order, USA.

III) The ethical issues are brought into the discussion in section IV on Common Witness. While not lifted explicitly by name, the bilaterals in this country touching abortion, euthanasia and human rights and the Faith and Order, USA, touching these themes and homosexuality are pioneering work that is decades away from being taken up in places like Germany and the Third World.

IV) Many Catholics will be surprised to find the universal ministry and primacy included in the agenda in Section Reports II and III, for the first time in a World Council context. Certainly the work of the Group des Dombes, the US Lutheran-Catholic dialogue and elements of the Anglican-Roman Catholic Final Report will be useful resources as the papacy becomes part of our common agenda, not only for study but also for reform!

4) The Spiritual mood of the Conference was dialogical and inclusive. The rules appeared initially (especially to some who had flown there not knowing we would not be allowed to speak! and who ended up keeping the rule while others seemed to ignore it) to be draconian. However, with the experience of Vancouver, Canberra and the Faith and Order plenary of Budapest under my belt, I was pleasantly surprised that so much work was able to be done, with such inclusive and fresh leadership and in such a short time. Of course, we are frustrated with the ecumenical process until the Church will be united (and I expect beyond!), but there appeared to be genuine engagement in the groups and genuine attempts in the section to redraft until the concerns of all of the duly appointed delegates were incorporated. Where differences are stated, there is a balance that enables us to go back to the churches, whatever their point of view, and demonstrate that there was no attempt of one church to dictate to another what its confessional position must be. While this lack of consensus is always painful, as a witness to the sinfulness of our division, its fair formulation is in itself a step forward creating the condition for reconciliation.

A theme from Archbishop Torella's opening homily to Konrad Raiser's articulating a vision for the future was that of "conversion." In the message and throughout the Section Church, of the communities that make up the Church and of the ecumenical movement, was a pervasive spiritual motif. Indeed, the advantage of such an international, multicultural meeting is to be able to listen to those theologies and cultures most different from one's own.

Again, the work of the Group des Dombes is an important contribution to the theological background of this theme – and a debate on the message shows, there is not yet a clear and common understanding of how it might apply to the Church itself – creature of God, empowered by the Holy Spirit and embodying the Risen Christ in the world as some of us confess.

5) The hopes for the US churches and for the ecumenical structures here are manifold, but let me just enumerate a few for our discussion:

I) Moderator Kishishian reiterated the theme of reception, a reception that implies a whole series of conversions:

a) a conversion in the way we do theology, confessionally, as individuals and in our preaching – presuming not that we are divided, which we are, but that we are in real, but perfect koinonia – using the results of the bilaterals, Faith and Order and church union work as central theological texts in our writing, teaching and catechesis – taking account our public witness, internal theological formulations and spiritual development of our leaders and people.

b) a conversion in our pastoral life, taking account of the Lund principle not only in common action – where it has yet to be fully received – but also in our common witness – speaking to the world together a common word, when not required by conscience to speak separately. This conversion will require an intense ecumenical formation at the highest level of those changed with oversight in our churches and with formulating its witness.

c) a conversion in the internal contemplative and prayer life of our churches, so that worship is incomplete without the ecumenical dimension, at whatever level is possible.

II) Again following Kishishian and the message, seeing to it, in our churches, in our ecumenical work and in our efforts as theologians that the bilateral and multilateral results are cöordinated and mutually reinforcing. The World Council, in its own way, generated the bilateral dialogues. Some have seen them as competitive. In this Conference the churches clearly affirmed their mutuality and interdependence.

III) The common vision by the churches of ecumenism as a whole: common mission, the quest for visible unity and collaboration at all levels.

IV) I see the proposals generated by a group of churches or by a pair of churches as ecclesiological contributions to the whole. I will pray for the fruitfulness – I don't think "success" is a particularly Christian word, or adequate description of what is a response to the grace of God and not good works – of such proposals as COCU, the Lutheran-Episcopal Concordat, or the full communion proposals before Lutheran and Reformed churches. While my Church may not be involved – juridically – in one or another proposal (all of these) spiritually there is as much at stake for the whole Christian family as for any church. It is a common spiritual journey.

V) US churches will have to begin to take history more seriously – *all* Christian history. This is not only in their seminary and college contexts, but also in the catechetical material and preaching.

VI) US ecumenical structures will have to reflect on what it means to be more inclusive with Orthodox, Pentecostal, Roman Catholic and other evangelical groups, along with the generous and long suffering "ecumenical" Protestant churches;

African, Asian, Middle Eastern, Latin American and minorities in all of our cultures as equals. The July 1993 issue of *Ecumenical Review* might be interesting reading in this regard.

Certainly, the increased intentional work on Faith and Order study and evaluation in these local and regional contexts will enrich the fabric of the ecumenical enterprise and forge bonds between the academic specialists, church leadership and grassroots communities in the one ecumenical enterprise.

6) This is the fifth such report that I have given and I find myself enriched each time by the diversity of responses from my colleagues who saw the World Conference from a different ecclesial and theological vantage point with a different set of expectations. (I suspect my most vivid memories will touch on conversations with a younger theologian about the African Synod, with an Australian woman minister about hermeneutics, with a South African Anglican bishop about how sexual debates are dealt with in that context, with a Philippine Jesuit about the ecumenical challenges in a predominantly Catholic Asian context, with a British Congregationalist about the new conciliar structures there, a Singaporean Pentecostal about Chinese inculturation, and American Mennonite about how to begin to understand Spanish piety, a Czech Orthodox woman about the differences in ecumenical relations between Slovakia and the Czech Republic, an Argentinean Dominican about how to "convert" CELAM and the structures of "old" Catholicism in Latin America, with an Australian Orthodox about tensions among the Greek speaking Orthodox, with the generous local Spanish folk receiving pilgrims in the villages of Castille about what "ecumenism" is when they will probably never talk to a non-Catholic in their lifetime etc.) We are on a

centuries-long road toward full reconciliation of the Church –
we have made dramatic progress since my Church came on
boards 25 years ago, and in the decades ahead Santiago will
stand as an important marker on the pilgrimage towards full
communion in faith, life and witness.

Santiago:
An Orthodox Perspective

Rev. Milton B. Efthimiou

WCC AND THE ORTHODOX: A SHORT HISTORY

When the WCC in Canberra decided to adopt the concept of Koinonia/Communion to describe the unity we seek as Christians in our joint efforts in Faith and Order, for many of the Orthodox this was the most significant action taken since the merging of the two major components of the Ecumenical Movement, i.e. when "Faith and Order" and "Life and Work" came together in 1948. For many action, which also gave impetus to what happened in Santiago, embodied what the Ecumenical Patriarchate had in mind when it issued the Patriarchal and Synodical Encyclical of 1902, addressed to Patriarchs and Heads of Orthodox Autocephalous Churches in matters "concerning our present and future relations with the two great bodies of Christianity, of the Roman Catholics and that of the Protestants," and the second Encyclical, of an ecumenical nature, issued in 1920 "unto all the Churches of Christ, wherever they may be," which became, in the words of Prof. Istavridis of the Ecumenical Patriarchate, "the constitution for the policy to be followed by the Orthodox Church in the Ecumenical Movement."[1] These two documents defined the relationship of the Orthodox which should exist among all Christians, and the extent to which all ecumenical activity should exist among all churches who always act together in one organization in

---

[1] V. Istavridis, "The Ecumenical Patriarchate and the WCC" in *The Greek Orthodox Theological Review*, IX (1963), p. 28.

collaboration of service to the world. Dr. Nikos Nissiotis, a pioneer of the Ecumenical Movement, called this, in his familiar phrase, the *"diakonia"* of churches that think and act together, regardless of their confessional differences, on the basis of Christian faith. For the Orthodox at Santiago, as just it was for the first Orthodox delegation led by the great theologian and ecumenist, Germanos, the Metropolitan of Thyateira, England, and on through the concise and memorable statements issued by Orthodox delegations on the occasion of the *major* ecumenical gatherings at Lausanne in 1927; Edinburgh in 1937; Evanston 1954; New Delhi in 1961; San Antonio in 1988, and Canberra in 1991; and in authoritative reports such as the one coming out of the Valamo Consultation (1977) on *"The Ecumenical Nature of the Orthodox Witness,"* as well as the Third Pre-Conciliar Pan-Orthodox Conference in 1986 on *"The Orthodox Church and the Ecumenical Movement,"* the message was, and is, always the same, consistently and fervently: *The aim of all ecumenical activity is the restoration of full communion among all Christians and all Churches.* In other words, the messages emanating from all these Conferences mentioned, which serve as guidelines for the Orthodox of every generation who participate in the WCC, is the affirmation, loud and clear, that Christian disunion is a scandal and contrary to what we pray in ancient Eucharistic Liturgies Sunday after Sunday in all Orthodox Churches throughout the world from time immemorial: "Let us pray to the Lord for the peace of the world, the stability of the Holy Churches of God and for the union of all!" – to put it down more succinctly, whether you draw from Lausanne, New Delhi, Canberra, or Santiago, the message, in various forms, is the same: guided by scripture and tradition, we affirm our obligation to seek to overcome misunderstandings and doctrinal differences which have contributed to the disunity of Christians. This also implies that the Orthodox of every generation affirm their responsibilities to join other Christians of good will in appropriate councils, forums and consultations which seek to overcome misunderstanding, to heal divisions and to foster unity in the Faith of the Apostles of Christ. The Ecumenical Patriarchate has always followed this line of thinking consistently in providing all Churches with inspiration and wisdom in these efforts of reconciliation, as well as in the challenge of dialogue with other Christians. Listen to the message of His All Holiness Bartholomew, the Ecumenical Patriarch of Constantinople, to the Conference and delegates of the Fifth World Conference on Faith and Order:

> It is our sincere hope that your common consideration of Koinonia in Faith, Life and Witness, may add decisively to all our previous efforts to receive together the divine gift of church unity, so that diversity among us may cease to be divisive and become, as at Pentecost, a living witness to the same redemptive reality.

What the Patriarch says echoes what I believe is the most concise statement on Church unity made in modern times, and, in many ways, the precursor of Orthodox participation at Santiago. It reminds me of what was stated at Chambesy in November 1986, during the Third Panorthodox Preconciliar Conference:

> The Orthodox participation in the Ecumenical Movement today is not foreign to the history of the Orthodox Church. It constitutes another endeavor to express the Apostolic faith in new historical situations and to respond to the new existential demands.[2]

[2] *Episkepsis*, #369, 1986, p. 14.

What this meant for the Orthodox, echoing voices of the past, was a mandate to always witness to the faith and tradition of the One, Holy, Catholic and Apostolic Church, which further means, to transmit that truth, as contained in Scripture and Tradition no matter what winds prevail at the time, what changes are taking place, so that the universal character of the church is kept intact, in spite of what the "socio-political shifts and changes of our times," in the words of Archbishop Iakovos, one of the pioneers of the Ecumenical Movement, who addressed Santiago with a message of stern admonition and counsel which reverberated throughout the plenary hall and within each discussion group.

Which leads us, in light of these preliminary remarks, to discuss what happened in Santiago.

SANTIAGO AND THE ORTHODOX

Coming together at Santiago, I was struck by the different faith partners, the different ways that each looked at the various issues, the priorities which each gave to agendas that were important to their particular denomination, and which, at times, reflected the methodological differences which so often cause difficulties in the process of "convergence." How, you might ask, did we come together? How, and in what way did the Orthodox contribute to the process of reception? Another pioneer of ecumenism once wrote that Orthodox ecclesiology draws always from Christian experience, which is a process that leads to "dialogue and crystallization of doctrine under the presence and breath of the Holy Spirit."[3] Metropolitan Chrysostomos of Ephesus, who wrote these words in paraphrasing a whole legion of Orthodox Fathers who remind us

[3] "The Place of Orthodoxy in the Contemporary Christian World," (in Greek) in *Stachys* (July 1985), No. 68-85, p. 340.

that all who accept Christ and are baptized in His Name are brought into union with Christ, with each other, and with the Church every time and every place. And all this is founded upon the communion of the Holy Spirit whose function is to allocate spiritual gifts to each of us, establish ministries, and in the process bind the members together in the one body which is the *"Ekklesia,"* the Church. This is crucial for non-Orthodox to understand why Orthodox think the way they do, and sometimes make demands that may seem unreasonable.

At the end of the Conference, a message was drafted by the executive committee which was problematic in some areas for some Orthodox which I would characterize as more a problem of language, which again goes back to the whole concept of Koinonia as participation in the life of God through being joined to Christ by the power of the Holy Spirit. In this divine life Christians are made one with each other. What happens many times, as in Santiago, it is hard to find a language which allows the diverse thinking to affirm both the holiness of God' Church and the human limitations of the members of that Church.

Allow me to expand thinking with you in relation to Santiago. What I would like to do is share with you and lift up not so much the content of the documents, but some reflections on the implications of Orthodox theology which came out of these documents and working sessions in our quest for present and future Christian ecumenical partnership in Faith and Order.

Here I might refer to the thinking of someone who is not Orthodox but who knows the Orthodox better than anyone I know! He is sitting right up here: Paul Crow; who in a recent lecture "Ecumenism, Spirituality and the Dark Night of the Soul" delivered last year at San Francisco University said:

I am convinced the Ecumenical Movement today reflects a more hopeful future and a deeper spiritual dilemma . . . The Churches are being called by God to a deeper reality of our unity in Christ . . . Our crisis lies not in institutional goals, incomplete theological consensus or financial shortages, but in a superficial prayer *life and lack of spirituality* among the churches and their members."[4]

Let me juxtapose this very Orthodox statement, perhaps best summarized in the sermon of Archbishop Stylianos of Australia on Transfiguration Day, and the papers of Metropolitan John Zizioulas of Pergamon and Archbishop Iakovos. For the Orthodox the criterion for the lack of spirituality and/or prayer life is to be tested among the different views of the Church as local and universal and as found among the various Christian communions. For the Orthodox there is only one Church in God's plan for salvation. This one Church is present and manifested in every single local church throughout the Oikoumene. It is the same Ekklesia of Christ which is present in every local church and it is the same Holy Spirit which, since the Church's inception, gathers together the faithful in the one church and in each individual local church. If we understand this fundamental ecclesiological principle, then we will understand where the Orthodox are coming from when they dialogue in Santiago or elsewhere in ecumenical meetings, and why they would disagree on certain issues. Metropolitan John's magnificent paper, *"The Church and Communion"* introduces us to the concept of *"Koinonia Ecclesiology"* and lays the groundwork for understanding that any and all ecclesiological investigation of this local and/or universal church must examine both the christological and Holy Spirit dimen-

[4] In Mid-Stream, vol. 32, #1 (January 1993) pp. 2-3.

sions (i.e. pneumatology) which are found in traditional Christianity (i.e. holy scripture and the needs of the early church). The Fathers of the Church help us in this quest! Ignatius of Antioch affirms: *"Where Jesus Christ is, there is the Catholic Church"* (*To Smyrnaeans*, VII, 2); Irenaeus affirms *"Where the Church is, there is the Spirit, and where the Spirit is, there is the Church"* (*Adversus Haereses*, III, 24).

This Church that the Fathers speak of is understood by the celebration of the Eucharist in and among the eucharistic gathering. What the Zizioulas paper *"The Church and Communion"* helped us do at Santiago is introduce the concept of Koinonia/Communion for understanding how we as a conglomerate of many diverse local Churches should be seen in the unity of the one Churches. But this "convergence" (a word widely used at Santiago) of the conglomerates of Churches can only be manifested through the theological meaning of "Koinonia," a term (as we were reminded by Fr. Martin Parmentier, a priest of the Old Catholic Church) that is used 19 times in the New Testament. Now this suggests something further basic to our understanding of *koinonia* (again, I am paraphrasing the Zizioulas paper): In Orthodox theology it is the theology of the Trinity that provides the theological basis of this *koinonia* ecclesiology. As Professor Grigorios Larentzakis, an Orthodox delegate reminded everyone at Santiago, applying the whole question of Church unity as *koinonia* means that the doctrine of the Holy Trinity must serve as model and example of this communion ecclesiology.

Now does everyone agree with this Orthodox approach to ecclesial unity? No, of course not. Many churches found it very problematic to deal with this, or, in the words of the Final Message, "On the Way to Fuller Koinonia," to explore how to confess our common faith in the context of so many "Cultures and Religions," in a world torn by social and national conflicts. One of the moderators, Dr. Mary Tanner, emphasized in her message that the concept of "Visible Unity" is the goal of ecumenism. Churches of North India protested that this was impossible because unity must be sought in terms of persons, not doctrines and church polity. The Orthodox disagreed. "Visible Unity" must be dealt with doctrinally, because the focus of visible unity for the Orthodox is at the level of Eucharistic Sharing, something which is very problematic on a doctrinal level for Orthodox and non Orthodox. Fr. Gennadios Limouris, our Orthodox representative at Geneva on the WCC staff kept emphasizing this point, and he and I kept reminding our section (Section II) that sacramental *koinonia* for the Orthodox presupposes canon law and doctrine on essentials, a point stressed in the area of ordination of women to the ministry. Archbishop Iakovos called them "ill-advised" ordinations, and set the tone, in his paper, for the sections to deal with the question of "spirituality and prayer" that Paul Crow talks of, and the idea that nurturing relationships with one another sometimes goes beyond canon law and doctrine in terms of understanding historically how the whole process of "reception" was lived and practiced by the local church in which ecclesial elements of the *one*, Holy, Catholic and Apostolic Church are integrally present. Iakovos went a step further and warned all present from his vast experience in the WCC that we should never lose sight of the "quest to recover the oneness of Christendom." Women's ordination, "unprecedented activism" in areas such as politics and human rights in recent times go counter to this quest, and do nothing to help us recover that ecclesiology of communion which bilateral and multilateral conversations deal with constantly on the thorny questions such as common profession of faith, the sacramental life of the Churches and the role of ecclesial authority and primacy, which was the basis of the Raiser and Keshishian papers on relating doctrine to social ethics.

CONCLUSION

I hope I have given some insight and food for thought as to why the adoption of *koinonia*/Communion was for many Orthodox one of the most significant actions taken in the WCC. Whether or not a "convergence" on issues on "diversity" took place will be debated for a long time. But I am sure that many left Santiago with the same feeling I had: division in the Church is contrary to our Lord's will; division in the Church contributes vastly to the division of the human family of the world; division in the Church blesses and sanctifies a divided world, whether in the Middle East, Yugoslavia, Russia, South Africa etc. The basis of a key booklet of the Conference called "Costly Unity" put out by the "J.P.I.C."[5] gathering in Denmark in February 1993 was exactly the point we are emphasizing; that committing ourselves to the Gospel of Jesus Christ is going to mean a unity that is going to be very "costly" for each and every one of us. For the Orthodox this means adherence to the tenets of the Faith as found in Scripture and Tradition. But we say this in His Name, knowing that our quest is His quest, to recover the oneness of Christian community, in spite of our "diversity" as we seek fresh, new, creative responses in anticipation of God's coming Kingdom, on where we go from here.

[5] "Justice, Peace and the Integrity of Creation," Unit III of the WCC.

St. Photius the Great and Rome

Metropolitan Methodios of Pisidia

I express my thanks to you for according me the privilege to speak of the relations of Photius the Great, Patriarch of Constantinople (858-867 and 877-886), with the Roman Church. I will not sketch the personality of the man, nor deal with the particulars of his career; these have been fully discussed by many Protestant scholars.

Over the past three years I have treated this subject at length.[1] What I propose here is an assessment of the distinctive characteristics of the two worlds which were represented by Photius and the Popes of Rome Nicholas I the Great (858-867), Hadrian II (867-872), John VIII (872-882), Marinus (882-885) and Stephanus V (or VI; 885-891).

Those who have been engaged with the relations between Constantinople and Rome have judged Photius as the person

---

[1] Cf. Archbishop Methodios Fouyas, *The Ecclesiastical Diversification of the Greek and the Latins*. From the time of St. Photius to the Council of Florence (858-1439). A historical and theological analysis of the various stages in the development of the ecclesiastical relations of the two peoples. Athens, 1990 (in Greek). For an appraisal of this work see, among others, Prof. J.E. Rexine in *The Patristic and Byzantine Review*, vol. 10 (1991), pp. 71-75; Dr. Gregorios Oikonomakos in the review *Parnassos*, Vol. 33 (1991), pp. 407-409 (in Greek); E. P. Lekkos in the review *Ekklesia*, 15 Nov. – 1 Dec. (1991), pp. 651-652 (in Greek); D. Kousios, in the newspaper *Europaratiritis*, Brussels, April 1991, pp. 1 and 2.

mainly responsible for the Schism of the two Churches, which persists to this day; however, in the post-World War II period, Photius has come to be regarded as responsible only for the Schism that lasted four years. This later view has been supported by the well known Czechoslovak scholar, Professor Francis Dvornik.[2]

If this was indeed the case, then the re-established Schism between the two Churches would have been dissolved. Or, even if relations between the two Churches were severed, unity might have been restored; schisms usually were of a temporary nature, and nearly all that occurred in the ancient Church soon disappeared. Examples are: that which followed the condemnation of St. John Chrysostom by the Synod of the Oak in A.D. 403, and gave Pope Innocent I (401-407) occasion to break off relations with the Churches of Alexandria, Antioch and Constantinople; this schism lasted until the year A.D. 438. Another is the so-called Acacian Schism, brought about because Acacius as Patriarch of Constantinople (471-489) together with the Patriarchs of Jerusalem, Alexandria and Antioch, applying the principle of "economia," accepted the "Henotikon" of the Emperor Zeno. The reaction of Pope Felix III (483-492) to this decision of the Patriarchs, whom he condemned, precipitated a schism which lasted from 484 to 519. Yet a third example is the schism which resulted from the Lateran Council when Pope Martin I (649-655) condemned the Monothelite Patriarchs of Constantinople, Sergius, Pyrrhus and Paul II.

Anyone familiar with ecclesiastical disputes will realize that schisms of this kind are inevitable within the body of the Church and do not necessarily impute self-interest to the contending

[2] F. Dvornik, *The Photian Schism: History and Legend*, Cambridge 1948, reprinted 1970.

Church leaders. But as is common knowledge, historians tend to trace ecclesiastical history, often deliberately ignoring factors which would not make schisms inevitable. For there are schisms that arise without specific and grave cause, and do not lead inexorably to divisions within the Church, nor result in "holy war" against the schismatics. Such appears to have been the case of Meletios of Antioch (A.D. 381) whose break with Rome did not prevent him from presiding over the Second Ecumenical Council in that year, a Council which Rome itself recognizes as Ecumenical. In light of all this, we must look elsewhere for the reasons behind divisions in the Church.[3]

To search out the underlying causes of the division of the Church into Eastern and Western, we must return to the first three Christian centuries.

During this period we observe that the Greek language was the dominant element in the unity of the Church; it was the medium for all communication among the various ecclesiastical centers. It is a datum of history that the christianization of the Roman Empire is attributable to the "hellenization" of the Christian religion, providing the fundamental force to counteract Roman tyranny. With the faith as a weapon and the Greek language as the medium, the Greeks gave Hellenism a new dimension; and they employed the wisdom and democratic concepts of their ancestors to form the basis of the Ecclesiastical Empire that would come to be known as "Oecumene."

It is my opinion that the term "Oecumene" was intended as a substitute for the title "Roman Empire," something which the Popes understood, hence their extreme reaction when the

---

[3] Documentation of my views and statements in this lecture may be found in my works, *Greeks and Latins*, and *An Introduction to St. Photius* (in Greek), published in the review *Ekklesia and Theologica*, vol. X (1991), pp. 1-126.

Patriarch of Constantinople added to his ecclesiastical acclamation (*pheme*) the title "Oecumenikos."

At the outset the Greeks adopted "Roman" as an ethnic identification, and they maintained that appellation in the sense that it identified them with the legacy of world-wide dominion with Constantinople as its center, while the ecclesiastical use of the term "Oecumenikos" displaced the term "Roman."

This consciousness of the Greeks as to the meaning of the term "oecoumenikos" was preserved in the office of the Ecumenical Patriarch, signifying the survival of both theories. However, there is a difference between "Romios" and "Romiosene," both terms enjoying currency largely during brief periods of a decline of the Greek State, or whenever the Byzantine Emperors felt the need to remind the people that Rome lay within the sphere of their Imperial dominion. These terms, "Romios" and "Romiosene," contended against the term "Hellene," though the latter prevailed ultimately as the Attic idiom predominated among all other dialects of the Greek language. Apart from all this, we must note the emergence of Roman Primacy (*proteion*) over against the rise of Greek ecumenicity (*pankosmiotita*). It must be acknowledged that the advancement of Roman Primacy is nothing but a reaction against a perceived Greek hegemony over the entire Christian Church.

The persecutions of the Christians by the Roman Emperors aimed at the extermination of that organized Hellenism which had restored spiritual vigor to the institutions of the Christian Church. The Roman Emperors feared the establishment of the Church with its bishops at her very center. For while the bishops had been separated from each other within local ecclesiastical provinces and effectively confined to these centers, they were nevertheless united in a spiritual unity with eschatological expectations. Such a center, though without any particular identity, was the Church of Rome, which was unmistakably Greek in the first three centuries.

Roman Catholic authorities tend to ignore the Greek character of the ancient Church of Rome, even though it is generally recognized that the Bishops of Rome, her Clergy, her scholars and the majority of her followers spoke Greek. Indeed the Greek language was a key factor in the unity of the Church of Rome with other Churches, Latin being inadequate to the need to express all the metaphysical nuances of doctrine and the requirements of Greek philosophical structures.

Historic evidences indicate that the Greek influence on the Church of Rome began to disappear by the end of the third century A.D., though this does not mean that the Greek contribution to the flourishing of the Roman Church likewise disappeared.

To support this particular view, I refer to the examples of Tertullian, Cyprian, Arnobius and Novatian, who might not have composed their Latin works had the Church of Rome not assimilated the fruits of Greek ecclesiastical literature of the first three Christian centuries. The richness of the Church of Rome, from the early Christian era up to the time of Eusebius, attests to the spiritual and intellectual standing of the leadership of the Church of Rome and of its members, who were ethnically and culturally Greek.

Influenced by the distinctive merits of Leo I, the Great, Bishop of Rome A.D. 440-461, both as theologian and churchman, scholars have paid little attention to certain strategies in his activities which definitely colored all relations between the Churches of East and West, well after his time. To help clarify the polity of Leo in this context of East-West relations, I would simply note that he served for some time as Nuncio (*apokrisarios*) of the Bishop of Rome in Constantinople, the capital of the Greek Empire. During his stay he affected to despise all things Greek – customs, traditions, even the Greek language which, as a consequence, he was unable to speak or understand.

Other surprising aspects of his activity aside, it was Leo who instituted and championed Roman Primacy (Proteion). In de-hellenizing the Church, he altered her very character, stamping upon her a Roman identity in all things. And acting on his own authority he imposed his claims on Constantinople and the Byzantine State in the reign of Marcian and Pulcheria, and on the Church itself through his representatives, presiding in his name over the Fourth Ecumenical Council of Chalcedon (A.D. 451).

Leo exercised tremendous influence over the participants at the Council of Chalcedon, and the approval of the "Tome of Leo," perceived as stating the authentic doctrine defining the two natures in the person of Christ, was adopted as a natural consequence. All this was due to the superficiality of the Emperors and the timidity of the Patriarch Anatolius in permitting the direct attack of Leo's deputation on the Alexandrian Church.[4] This policy of Rome represents the first explicit endeavor to humiliate the Eastern Church and to reduce her power; in consequence the Eastern Orthodox Church has for nearly fifteen centuries remained estranged from Rome. And as a consequence of the decisions of Chalcedon, the Armenians, the Copts, the Syrians and the Ethiopians were cut off

---

[4] The loss of Egypt was a fatal stroke to Byzantine civilization because the seizure of Alexandria eliminated Hellenism as the source of Greek learning, which Alexandria had been until the early 7th century A.D..

from the Eastern Orthodox Church. These disastrous developments cost the Byzantine Empire extensive fertile areas which never returned to the jurisdiction of the Byzantine Emperor or the spiritual authority of the Orthodox Patriarchs of the East. All these areas were conquered by Arab warriors who succeeded in an astonishingly short time to extend their sovereignty as far as Persia in the East and ultimately to Spain in the West.

In the wake of all these unhappy events, whenever the Orthodox Church sought to achieve an accommodation with the Oriental Churches, they were confronted with the obstructive reaction of Rome. In time, ignoring the Greek Church altogether, Rome instituted the "Unia," destined to become the most divisive element of all in the relations between the Churches.

But there must be yet another reason why the Roman Church was able to achieve such development at the expense of the Greek Church. And that was the Imperial policy in Byzantium which always desired to have the Pope at its side. The Emperor of Byzantium lived under the delusion that Rome was a part of his Empire; hence the practice of applying the leverage which the Pope provided to help neutralize the power of the Patriarchs of Constantinople. For their part the Popes were more than willing to overshadow the position of the Patriarchs of Constantinople. Thus the Popes served the interests of the Byzantine Emperors while at the same time buttressing their claims to primacy, "judged of no one," as it was often stated. The role of the Byzantine Emperors proved to be the catalyst insofar as compromising the independence of the Byzantine Church; its history is replete with examples of dethronement by force and the humiliation of Patriarchs. I mention the cases of Ignatius, Photius, Michael Cerularius, Arsenius, Ioannis Beccos and Joseph I. These examples represent the saddest of injustices, which explains the numerous studies that have appeared on these men. All these studies arrive at a common conclusion: that Caesaropapism did not exist in Byzantium. This is not true. The truth is that there were Patriarchs unwilling to tolerate the expansion of the Emperor's domination of the Church's affairs, but the price for integrity invariably was the loss of the Patriarchal throne.

This policy of Imperial Byzantium in turn led to many humiliations of the Church of Constantinople by Rome. The Roman Popes recognized *de facto* the sovereignty of the Emperor whenever the question of union of the two Churches was raised. It was the Emperor, not the Patriarch, whom the Pope sought as his ally. The result was that all such efforts concluded in pseudo-unions.

The form of Caesaropapism which was brought to Byzantium from Rome is the one characteristic of Byzantine life which survived to the end of the Byzantine Empire and, in yet another form, was perpetuated by the Tsars of Russia and the Sultans of the Ottoman Empire.

Some balance was struck by the Patriarch Photius in his *Epanagogé*, which draws a distinction between the two authorities. The aim of Photius' *Epanagogé* was to define the rights and obligations of Emperor and Patriarch respectively.[5] But the distinction was moot when the two principals disagreed; inevitably the loser was the Patriarch who was expelled from his throne, leaving the Emperor free to pursue his own purposes. It can hardly be denied that from the very beginnings of the Byzantine Empire, that is, from the reign of Constantine the Great, to the last Emperor to deal with the issue of union

---

[5] Cf. Sp. Trojannos, "Photius the Great and the Order of the Esiagogé: Some remarks regarding the relations of Church and State," *Ekklesia and Theologia*, vol. X (1991), pp. 489-504.

at Florence, it was the Emperor who controlled the Church's policy and was the authority which dictated it. It would be frivolous and less than candid to deny that Caesaropapism as a system was operative in the relations of Church and State in Byzantium. The pattern having been set by Constantine, it was never forgotten in Byzantium, even though Constantine's successors by and large never assumed control of Church affairs to the same extent. The case of Leo VII, who expelled Photius the Great in order to elevate his brother Stephanus to the throne, and that of Romanus Lecapinus (920-944) who appointed his son Theophylactus as Patriarch at the age of 16, suffice to assess the various theories of *inter-relational* or of *patronization* advanced by those who have studied relations between Church and State in Byzantium.

After the ninth century the Emperors ceased to intervene in doctrinal issues; they did not, however, stop driving the Church into pseudo-unions with Rome. Some of them secretly, others openly, adopted the Roman Catholic faith.[6] Numerous attempts have been made to justify such conversions on the premise that imperial intervention into the Church's affairs would thus be seen as praiseworthy. Nonetheless, the intervention of the Emperor – as in the case of Theodosius II, Pulcheria, Marcian and Anastasius I – was of great significance.

When Charlemagne wanted to exercise control over the Church, it was Byzantine Caesaropapism that he adopted, particularly that of the iconoclast Emperors. But his intentions encountered the strong reaction of Popes Hadrian I (771-795) and Leo III (795-816), who defended the Seventh Ecumeni-

---

[6] J. Gill, "Eleven Emperors of Byzantium Seek Union with the Church of Rome," in *Eastern Churches Review*, vol. IX (1977), pp. 72-84.

cal Council, a fact that Photius mentions with gratitude in his *Mystagogia.*

While it is true that there were instances of complete control of ecclesiastical affairs by the Emperors of Byzantium, there were also, as we have seen, exceptions, when the Patriarchs of Constantinople preferred humiliation over submission to the Emperor. Circumstances enabled the Popes of Rome to prevail over political authority. However, the view of the great scholar Father Dvornik is less accurate when he states: "Of course we did admit that there were some Eastern Fathers who gallantly fought for orthodoxy of faith; but had it not been for the intervention of the Popes, the whole East would have sunk bodily into heresy."[7] Dvornik's statement is an exaggeration, as is proved by the positions taken by the Patriarchs Photius the Great and Michael Cerularius against both Rome and the Byzantine State. They consistently defended the faith and the jurisdictional integrity of the Ecumenical Patriarchate against Rome and the political authority.

The dispute over Bulgaria and South Italy appears to have been a quarrel over the Ecumenical Imperium because of the German and Norman threat, and the defense and protection of the Orthodox faith was imperative. But on the whole the policy of the Byzantine Emperor's regarding the Church had political motives, and the Popes always grasped the opportunity to exploit it.

This subject has been researched by Joseph Gill in the context of the history of Byzantium; he states unequivocally that the approaches of the Byzantine Emperors to the Papacy were always politically motivated. The Popes for their part exploited the difficult position of the Greek Empire and consistently

[7] "The Study of History and Christian Reunion," *Eastern Churches Quarterly*, vol. VI (1945), p. 18.

pressed upon the Greeks their claim of the primacy of the Roman See and the Roman Pontifex Maximus; they demanded obedience to every Pope successively canonically elected to the Papal office. In addition they stipulated for all Christians free appeal to Rome, devotion to the Pope as holding first place in the Councils, and approval of papal decisions except when these were clearly uncanonical.

It must be said, however, that these papal claims never became acceptable to the leadership of the Greek Church. European scholars treating the issue of Byzantine political leadership vis-a-vis the Church, take a somewhat idealistic stance, because the Emperors of the West were more oppressive to the Church.

The motives behind the conflict between the two great Church leaders, Photius and Nicholas I, should be traced within the spirit which prevailed in the Byzantine Empire and the manner in which relations between Rome and Constantinople had developed. During this period Greek self-complacency, as A. Ehrhard calls it,[8] regarded itself as immeasurably superior to the West. Photius' defiant stand against papal authority reflected the hauteur of the whole nation as a result of the establishment of the Western Empire. According to H. Gelzer,[9] Photius was destined to defend the Greek nation against the claims of Rome as these were now being advanced with ever greater persistence and finesse. Referring to Rome at this time, he states that if Rome had actually possessed the political prudence which scholars so often and so uncritically attribute to her, she ought to have done a turnabout. Photius was resolute in defending against Rome the spiritual independence of the Greek nation. This is the historical meaning of his Encyclical Letter in A.D. 867. Having been emancipated from Rome

[8] *History of Byzantine Literature*, vol. I (1897), p. 139.
[9] ibid. vol. III (1900), pp. 355-377.

nearly half a millennium before, by virtue of the titanic efforts of Photius, the Greek nation now enjoyed its ecclesiastical liberation as well. This success represents Photius' greatest and most enduring achievement, Gelzer maintains.

But Photius was to have cordial relations with a later Pope, John VIII, of whom he speaks with considerable affection. Some Roman Catholic writers charge John with cowardice, which may have served as inspiration for Baronius in fabricating the legend of the female Pope John. But the story is not so. According to H. Gelzer, Pope John was a capable and rather cunning person, though Photius proved to be more skillful than his adversary in his dark intrigues. However, in all of this we should tread with caution as the truth is not always treated with reverence.

The Greeks were in fact, in many respects, superior to the Latins. Hence the inevitable conflict with Rome and the emancipation of the Greeks from Rome's Primacy. Accordingly, Photius fulfilled the political as well as the ecclesiastical program admirably. My aim in citing these historical events is to cast a different light on them than that under which many historians have viewed and presented them.

The transfer of the Capital of the Roman Empire from the Old Rome to the New Rome did not mean the automatic decline in the splendor of the Old Rome; nor was it the intention of the Emperors of Byzantium, in their political aims, to abdicate their sovereignty over the West. On the one hand this policy sustained the ambitions of the Pope of Rome. On the other hand it reduced the Greek Church to second class. For this reason alone the work of Photius and Michael Cerularius has overriding historical significance. Numerous books have been written in an effort to interpret the position of these two great Church leaders against the expanding pretensions of the

Popes of Rome. In the end it must be confessed that this contest resulted in the calamities visited upon the Greeks by the Crusades, the dissolution of the Byzantine Empire by the Ottomans, and the implementation of *Unia* by Rome, aiming at the submission of the Orthodox Church to the Church of Rome.

I will close this lecture by citing two important events which accentuate the relations between the Church of Rome and the Orthodox Church.

The Council of 879-80 is an event of great significance for both Churches. Representatives of Pope John VIII were present at that Council, where harmonious relations between the two Churches were restored. It is regrettable that the Church of Rome has not recognized this Council as Ecumenical and not listed it among the Ecumenical and Holy Councils of the One and undivided Church of the first eight centuries. To the contrary, Rome has recognized as Ecumenical the Council of 869-70, which condemned the Patriarch Photius to degradation and deposed him. Various scholars have engaged in the study and interpretation of these two events according to their respective prejudices. Particularly as regards the Council of 879-80, it is alleged that Photius forged the letters of Pope John to serve his own purpose, while the Pope was misunderstood by the Church of Rome because of his friendly attitude towards Photius and was blamed, unjustly, for lacking the strength of a man. The truth is that both parties were well-disposed towards reconciliation and in this respect were totally sincere. If these events, indeed the whole state of affairs, had been properly assessed, the Church would have continued united, despite all the particularities that existed on both sides.

Today the position of Photius in history is regarded as a hopeful phenomenon: Roman Catholic scholars tend to soften the enmity against him and to raise the possibility of recognizing the Photian Council as Ecumenical. Lacking such recognition, there would seem to be little hope of restoring unity between the separated Churches of East and West. The case of Photius still awaits the objective judgement of Rome regarding the Ecumenicity of the Council of 879-80, wisely approved by Pope John VIII.

Recently it has been suggested that Photius had accepted, or at least not rejected, Roman Primacy. As to this issue it must be borne in mind that the Orthodox Church does not connect the leading role of St. Peter amongst the Apostles with any of those Churches which he founded or served. For while it is true that St. Peter was the leading figure amongst the Apostles, this leadership did not devolve upon the bishops of any Church. Moreover, the first place occupied by the Bishop of the Church of Rome in Ecumenical Councils was accorded him not *ex officio*, or because St. Peter was the first Bishop of Rome, but because such was the decision of the Councils, to allot the presidency to the Bishop of Rome as *primus inter pares*, a thesis that continues to be maintained by the Eastern Orthodox Church.

It goes without saying that Photius accepted the principle of *pentarchia*, i.e. the collegial authority of the five ancient Patriarchates, implying as it did a primacy of honor for the Bishop of Rome, but totally unrelated to the claim of Papal Primacy. This at any rate is the conclusion drawn by students of Church history, which explains why he is so fiercely attacked. He was seen as an enemy of Roman Primacy not only by Roman Catholic scholars, but by Luther, Calvin, Melanchthon and other leaders of the Reformation.

The fact that in his letters to the Bulgarians Photius does not mention Rome, placing her first with respect to the other Thrones, is evidence of his view that the Church of

Constantinople had precedence in fact over the Church of Rome. Whether he is on good terms with the Emperor of Byzantium or not, all his ecclesiastical and leadership efforts are aimed at neutralizing the notion of Roman Primacy; he considered it inimical to the interests of the Church and the Greek positions (theses).

It is unfortunate that Father Dvornik seeks grounds for his assertion that Photius accepted Papal Primacy. Photius does in fact speak highly of the Church of Rome, but rather in the nature of flattery, which I believe he thought expedient for the sake of ecclesiastical unity. He did so also because he lived in a similar climate of hauteur which prevailed amongst the Greeks.

It is evident, then, that any notion that Photius supported Roman Primacy is utterly groundless; had he in fact recognized Rome's jurisdiction over the whole Church, he would hardly have ventured to condemn Pope Nicholas I and declare him deposed in 867. Moreover, in his letter of that year, inviting Church leaders to participate in the forthcoming Ecumenical Council, Photius demonstrates his belief in the synodical system of the Christian Church.

The other thorny problem that embittered the relations of the churches is the *Unia*, regarded as the most acute expression of the ecclesiastical conflict between Greeks and Latins. Its enforcement, in ways that are seen as often unchristian and inhumane, resulted from Rome's failure to subject the Greeks ecclesiastically and to force acceptance of the decisions of the Councils of Lyons and Florence.

The establishment of a Uniate institution within the bosom of the Orthodox Church, and of other Oriental Churches as well, is viewed as a distinctly unchristian aspect of the relations between the Latins and the Greeks and Eastern Christendom as a whole. However, as an attempt it remains unjustified and unfulfilled. The expectations of the Papacy, that the democratic Greek Church would become subject to the hegemony of Rome, have not been realized.

This device, which cost the lives of many ordinary people, both conscientious if cunning Roman missionaries and Orthodox faithful in various regions of Poland, Czechoslovakia, Romania and Yugoslavia, as well as in Ethiopia, is a phenomenon without a shred of justification in the teachings of the Church Fathers. Its motivation is altogether ulterior, betraying a hypocrisy which cannot be ignored today in our relations with the Roman Catholics. The problem of *Unia* emerged once the Popes realized that it was the last and only way the Orthodox world could be brought under the domination of Rome. Indeed it underlies the relations between Greeks and Latins. At the heart of this policy lies the fundamental aim of bringing the entire Christian world under the sway of the Popes of Rome.

The Roman Catholic Church is unable to live the Christian life in its ideal while separated from the Orthodox Church. And what Rome has consistently sought to achieve is union with the Greeks. What is surprising therefore to me in the case of *Unia* is how badly the Roman Popes misjudged, ignoring how entrenched in their position the Greeks became as a result of the Crusades. In that crucial era the Greeks made it clear to all parties involved that they were not all disposed to compromise the Christian good of freedom of conscience, their most precious possession through those trying times. On that freedom the Greeks had based their very theology. Indeed on that freedom they based their dignity, at a time when some of their opportunist leaders took refuge in Rome, actually self-excommunicated.

In my work *Greeks and Latins,* I deal at length with the Institution of *Unia* and its expansion from its beginnings to the present day. I also refer to the sentiments of the disappointment of some leaders of that movement who lament having been cut off from the Orthodox Church.[10]

I wrote this work before the world-shaking changes in Eastern Europe where the *Unia* had its most impressive success. Notwithstanding this, I foresaw that the history of the Uniate Churches in the Ukraine and Romania had not ended as yet; that owing to the loosening of dictatorial measures in Eastern Europe, and the contacts of Russian religious and political leaders with the Vatican, there would be a change in the status of the Uniates in those area. This is precisely what has happened. *Unia* has revived anew, and in invading these regions anew, the Vatican has lent a new dimension to the Schism between Rome and Orthodoxy.

Understandably, the human factor has played a major role in the relations between East and West. For their part the Latins felt compelled to perpetuate the Roman concept of the Roman Pontifex Maximus in the office of the Pope, along with all the Christian tradition related to that office. The Greeks on the other hand sensed only a tenuous connection with world history. Nonetheless, after the Greco-Roman era both had a common starting point, that Greco-Christian tradition which developed throughout the Roman Empire This is their common legacy since no Latin Christianity per se existed before the evolution of Christian theology. This is of the greatest significance for both peoples, because this common legacy constitutes the meeting point for Greeks and Latins, Slavs and Franks. The creative contact of Christianity with the stable ideas of the Greek tradition formed a matrix similar to that of Alexandria when two universal systems, Hellenic civilization

---

[10] *Greeks and Latins*, op. cit. pp. 372-388.

and the Christian Church, were destined to merge, evolving the sound architecture of Alexandrian theology, as the renowned Scholar W. Jaeger so wisely observes in his splendid work, *Early Christianity and Greek Paedeia*. From Alexandria the developed Greek spirit, now melded with Christianity, passed on to Cappadocia, becoming the point of reference for all knowledge, piety, education, philanthropy, etc.

This synthesis created the norm of Christian learning, conduct and discipline which, until the fatal Schism, guided the One Church, of the Greeks and the Latins alike. Despite all the adversities the Greeks experienced, they never abandoned this spirit, a fact we cannot ignore whenever we encounter our Christian brothers. It survives in our modern world and may be hoped that with our growing participation in a United Europe, it may become a European virtue, all of Europe acquiring the spirit and discipline of Orthodoxy.

The Orthodox Church in Theological Dialogues

Metropolitan Methodios of Pisidia

The theological dialogues of the Orthodox Church with other Churches of the West and of the East represent for me familiar ground, having been connected with them both directly and indirectly.

While in Great Britain, and after completing post-graduate studies for the Ph.D. degree, twenty-five years ago, I wrote the work entitled: *Orthodoxy, Roman Catholicism and Anglicanism*, first published by Oxford University press in 1972, and later, in a second edition, by the Holy Cross Orthodox Press (Brookline, Massachusetts 1984). In the preface to the second edition I state unequivocally that " . . . I have not been able to convince myself that there will be any fundamental change between the Orthodox and Roman Catholic Churches for some time to come. I fear that the theological dialogue between the Churches will have no influence upon inter-church relations. The situation between the Orthodox and the Anglicans is growing worse due to the instability of the contemporary Anglican Church with respect to the catholic elements of the Church of Christ."

As Archbishop of Aksum I prepared and published another work entitled: *The Person of Christ in the Decisions of the Ecumenical Councils, with Special Reference to Oriental Orthodox Relations with Orthodoxy and Roman Catholicism*, published in Addis Ababa (Ethiopia) 1975. And very recently I published a

Survey under the title *Revolution towards Unity: Ecclesiastical and Theological Contacts among the Eastern Orthodox Catholic Church and the Oriental Orthodox Churches* (Athens 1991).

Within the limits of time which this lecture allows, I shall try to develop this broad subject, drawing on both personal experience and the writings I have just cited.

I should point out at the outset that a spirit of friendship and co-operation between Orthodox and Anglicans has existed for many centuries. This fact has prompted me to offer my full support, in affection, to the effort for mutual understanding and for closer ties of friendship between the two Churches.

There have been theological discussions at a rather academic level, held sporadically, to use the expression of the late Archbishop of Canterbury Michael Ramsey of blessed memory. In his words: "The relations between the Church of England and the Holy Orthodox Church, before the First World War, were informal and spasmodic; now they are far more frequent and on a number of occasions official." But the most interesting fact is that "the Church of England has never quarreled with the Orthodox Church. There is no rivalry, there are no catalogues of wrongs inflicted, no smoldering memories of religious wars, no feeling that the other's real purpose is to undermine one's position. In conversations between Anglicans and Presbyterians, or Anglicans and Roman Catholics, there are so many feelings, such a deep suspicion on all sides. When Orthodox and Anglicans meet, there is very little suspicion, very little temptation to get angry with them."[1]

Nevertheless, in the East, Anglicanism is regarded as a

---

[1] J. Lawrence – *Anglicans and Orthodox, Rediscovering Eastern Christendom.* Essays in memory of Dom Winslow, ed. by E.L.B. Fry and A.H. Armstrong, London, 1963, p. 120.

Protestant Church, albeit preserving pro-catholic elements such as the episcopacy. On the other hand, in England as much as elsewhere in the West, the Orthodox Church has been considered a dead branch of the ancient Church. It seems to me that some Orthodox scholars are under an illusion as to the real position of Anglicanism, regarding it as a Catholic Church in a state of reformation. Such was in fact the consensus among the Orthodox until today, based on the belief that the Anglican Communion retained many similarities with the Orthodox Church, in particular those which relate to its organization and its sacramental life. Very few Orthodox realize that Anglicanism is intellectually and in its ethos closer to the Romans than to the Orthodox, although they are being strongly influenced by the Greek Church Fathers. And despite the fact that there are within Anglicanism strikingly Protestant elements, these do not constitute any obstacle to unity with the Roman Catholic Church.

The old state of affairs, when Anglicanism was divided into three irreconcilable parties, no longer exists. Moreover, we must not underestimate the great importance given by Anglicanism to Christian unity, nor the fact that discussions on unity are carried on by representatives of all shades of opinion rather than of a single group within the Anglican Church as has been the case in the past.

The Orthodox Church maintains the firm position that her teaching has been formulated in accordance with the decisions of the Ecumenical Councils and is not prepared to deviate from them. This thesis is unacceptable to the Anglicans, having developed a view similar to that of the Roman Catholic Church. I am inclined to believe that the Anglicans did not take kindly to the declaration of Patriarch Meletios of Alexandria when he said at Lambeth in 1930: "We shall discuss not our teaching, but question whether the Anglican Church is or can be in agreement with the Orthodox Church."

Although Anglicans admire the Orthodox Church for its defense of the Christian faith and Christian doctrine, they meet them as brothers and children of the same God, as members of the same body in the name of our Lord Jesus Christ. But what Anglicans and other Protestants forget is that the safeguarding of the Truth is a fundamental principle of action for Orthodoxy. Its Constitution provides the material for the defense of the Christian Faith and the decisions of the Ecumenical Councils, though this does not mean that new dogmatic formulas cannot be issued by future Ecumenical Councils.

Anglo-Orthodox discussions were held at Lambeth (1930), in Bucharest (1935), and in Moscow (1956). At the Lambeth Conference the Anglican Bishops favored relations with the Orthodox at the expense of their relations with their fellow-countrymen. Dr. Visser't Hooft, the General Secretary of the World Council of Churches, said that before the last war, the Church of England had a "maximum program" of reunion for the Orthodox, and a "minimum program" for the Protestants.

As a result of the visit of Dr. Fisher, then Archbishop of Canterbury, to the Ecumenical Patriarchate in 1960, and in response to his request, the Ecumenical Patriarchate decided to set up a commission charged with continuing the doctrinal discussions of the Joint Anglo-Orthodox Committee of 1930-31, which had been interrupted by the onset of World War II.

In November, following appropriate study, the Third Pan-Orthodox Conference authorized the immediate formation of an Inter-Orthodox Theological Commission and requested the various Orthodox Churches to appoint their own representatives for the preparation of the Theological Dialogue with the Anglicans, based on consultations that had been held with the Anglican Church.

As a consequence of the Rhodes Conference in 1964, meetings of the Inter-Orthodox Theological Commission were held in Belgrade September 2-15, 1966, to draw up the agenda for the Anglican-Orthodox Dialogue.

The Belgrade discussions among the Orthodox made it clear that the Orthodox have somewhat confused ideas about the Anglican Church. It was further observed that the two Churches have different points of departure, making problematic the reconciliation of their differences. The Anglicans start from the Bible, though sometimes ignoring the traditional way of interpreting it, whereas the Orthodox faithfully carry on the life of the Church through the centuries. On the other hand, the Orthodox do not fully understand the prevailing spirit in Anglican thought. For example, they cannot quite grasp the term "comprehensiveness" and of course do not translate it correctly.

After long and fruitful discussions together, the two Theological Commissions issued a communiqué, largely confined to mutual compliments.

It seems fitting at this point to cite the fundamental principle, stated by the Patriarch Photius the Great in his letter to Pope Nicholas I, as normative for the Orthodox Church, but to which we give scant attention: "If the question has nothing to do with faith, or is not related to a universal decision, that is to say, has not been taken by an Ecumenical Council, but relates only to customs and usages, then blameworthy is he who would deem wrongdoers those who follow them, or condemn those who abstain from them." "There are things which are common to all; I mean those which must be observed by all, above all others those which relate to faith, deviation from which approaches sin, which leads to death, and for some it is truly sin . . . ."

Since 1970 I have been a member of the Orthodox Theological Commissions which held several sessions, both separately and together with the Anglicans. Yet in spite of all these efforts, on both sides, nothing was achieved for the promotion of unity of the two Churches. Since 1980 I have acted as President of the Orthodox Theological Commission, and apart from the development of friendly relations between the two Churches, the results of the meetings of the two Theological Commissions were much as before. The reason the efforts have not borne fruit is the problem which has emerged within the Anglican Communion over the ordination of women to the priesthood, also the public declaration of Dr. Jenkins, the Bishop of Durham, rejecting the divinity of our Lord Jesus Christ. I was fortunate in managing to salvage the dialogue at a very critical moment in the meeting of Anglicans and Orthodox in Dublin, at which time the representatives of the Orthodox Churches of Russia and Greece demanded that the dialogue be terminated.

One of the fundamental characteristics of Anglicanism is its variety of traditions and schools of thought. It is the reason that there is no agreement among them as to the position they must hold on intercommunion. The Evangelical and Liberal traditions take a favorable position and would be ready to accept intercommunion with all who believe sincerely in our Lord Jesus Christ. But for intercommunion between Orthodox and Roman Catholics unity in faith is the essential prerequisite.

Relations between the Orthodox and Roman Catholics are a sad story of conflicts and estrangement between Greeks and Latins. I have dealt with them at length in my book *Greeks and Latins*, as I stated in the first of these lectures.

The beginning of the confrontation between Rome and Constantinople coincides with the pontificate of Leo the Great

(440-461). Leo aimed at the separation of the Eastern Church as well as the consolidation of his Primacy – indeed the Primacy of the Roman Church over all Christendom – and accordingly established the Latin Church of Rome after a protracted struggle with Constantinople.

The sharp ecclesiastical differences that had developed between the two Churches were revealed in the events following the elevation of Photius to the Ecumenical Throne (858-867 and 877-886) and of Nicholas I (858-867). Both men, who emerged as "great' out of the events which they shaped, fought for the dominance of their ideas: Photius for the Orthodox faith and the independence of the Greek world and the ideals of its legacy; Nicholas for the Roman Imperium as embodied in the Primacy of the Pontifex of the Church of Rome over all of Christendom.

The clash of the two thrones, of Constantinople and Rome, culminated in the so-called Schism of 1054, during the patriarchate of Michael Cerularius (1049-1059) and the papacy of Leo IX (1049-1054). The impact of the Crusades upon the relations of the two Churches were far-reaching, while the outcome of the Councils of Lyons and Florence failed to resolve the differences which had kept the two Churches apart. The fall of Constantinople and the imposition of Ottoman rule over Christian Orthodox territories for four centuries assured the permanent division of the Church into East and West.[2]

In spite of all this hostility and conflict, Orthodoxy and

[2] While there are numerous commentaries and reviews of my book, *Greeks and Latins*, an English outline is added there. In addition, there is a lengthy review, also in English, in *The Patristic and Byzantine Review*, New York, vol. 10, 1991, pp. 71-75, written by Prof. John Rexine of Colgate University, to whom I here express my gratitude.

Roman Catholicism have affirmed that they will continue their efforts towards reconciliation.

The late Greek scholar and academician Hamilcar Alivizatos, writing in 1951 on the necessity of Christian dialogue, says that Orthodoxy and Roman Catholicism share the privilege of defending catholic principles in the Ecumenical dialogue. No other Church is as firmly committed to fidelity of tradition. No other Church is free of what both Catholics and Orthodox, in the light of the Great Councils, regard as heresies.

There are three factors which have impelled Orthodox and Roman Catholics toward rapprochement. The first is ease of communication, which today enables the Churches to converse. The second is the election to the Roman See of Pope John XXIII. The third is persistent and sincere effort for Christian unity of the late Patriarch Athenagoras of Constantinople. But the initiative towards unity of the two Churches, indeed of all the Churches, dates from 1920, when the Ecumenical Patriarchate appealed to "All the Churches of Christ wheresoever they be." This document, promulgated many years before the World Council of Churches was established, is regarded as one of the most significant early records of ecumenism; it demonstrates that the Patriarchate of Constantinople never ceased laboring for the fulfillment of Christ's will for the unity of the Church. Leo Zander, a Russian theologian and ecumenist, has called this Encyclical "The Golden Charter of Orthodox Ecumenism."[3]

According to the former General Secretary of the World Council of Churches, Dr. Visser't Hooft, the significance of

---

[3] The Encyclical Letter of the Ecumenical Patriarchate issued in 1920 was included in the *Documentation of Christian Unity* (1920-1924), ed. by Bishop G. Bell, London, 1924, No. 13, p. 44.

this Encyclical Letter is threefold: a) It shows that the Church of Constantinople was the first Church to decide officially to propose to the other Churches of Christ a permanent fellowship in a Council of Churches. b) Of further significance is that the Encyclical is addressed to all Churches in the world, to fellow-heirs, members of the same body, and partakers of the promise of Christ. c) Above all, the Church of Constantinople formulated an important principle by affirming in the Letter that the contacts which were thus being proposed should not be deferred until complete doctrinal agreement was reached, but that co-operation among the Churches would prepare the way for such unity.

It would be a serious omission if I were to overlook the great number of Encyclical Letters which the Popes of Rome addressed to the Eastern Church, [4] though the difference between Constantinople and Rome lies in the purpose of these initiatives. Whereas Constantinople speaks of Christian unity, Rome invariably invites the East to be united with the Roman Church under the Supreme Pontiff.

Encyclical Letters were also issued by the Patriarchs Meletios IV (1921-1923) and Athenagoras (1949-1972).

For many years the Romans and the Protestants maintained that the Orthodox Church could not convoke a Pan-Orthodox Council for the simple reason that she lacked primacy. Yet in spite of the difficulties arising out of the situation of the Orthodox Churches in Eastern Europe, in 1961 the first Pan-Orthodox was convened on the Island of Rhodes. There it was determined that the Orthodox Church should develop relations with the Roman Catholic Church.

Two years later, the second Pan-Orthodox Conference was

---

[4] See the List of Papal Encyclicals to the East in my book, *Greeks and Latins*, pp. 391-393.

convened, again on Rhodes, by the Ecumenical Patriarch Athenagoras, and it was decided to extend a proposal to the venerable Roman Catholic Church to enter into dialogue with the Orthodox Church on equal terms. This proposal was accepted by the Roman Catholic Church when Patriarch Athenagoras and Pope Paul VI met in the Holy Land (5-6 January 1964). A further outcome of this meeting was what could be regarded as a clear commitment on both sides to set up Commissions with the Roman-Orthodox dialogue as their mandate.

During the Third Pan-Orthodox conference of Rhodes (1964) a very important event took place. Cardinal Bea, President of the Secretariat for Christian Unity, arrived at the Conference carrying a personal message from Pope Paul. In his message the Pope compared the Pan-Orthodox Conference to the Vatican Council; in response the Ecumenical Patriarchate dispatched a delegation to the Vatican (14 February 1965), the first such delegation after many centuries of interrupted communication. The purpose was to apprise the head of the Roman Church of the decisions of the Third Pan-Orthodox Conference, thus creating a promising climate for the commencement of a fruitful theological dialogue.

In April 1965, a Roman Catholic delegation visited the Ecumenical Patriarch, again carrying a highly important message for Patriarch Athenagoras. The letter was a very significant document in that the Roman Catholic Church was acknowledging the identical intent of the two Churches concerning their mutual desire for unity. It was clear that the language of communication between the two Churches had changed. The Pope of Rome and the Ecumenical Patriarch began an exchange of letters in the spirit of Christian love and mutual esteem.

At the same time it should be noted that the observers of

the Dialogue between Roman Catholicism and Orthodoxy were from the very beginning divided as to their expectations from it. An official of the Vatican Council and the Office for Christian Unity writes: "The amelioration of social problems should take precedence, whereas others maintain that dogmatic problems must first be settled. But immediate results of the dialogue ought to take the form of co-operation and collaboration in practical matters." The late Professor G. Florovsky pointed out the danger that an efficient co-operation of divided Christians on social issues, or in the field of international affairs, can obscure, or even destroy, the vision of true Christian unity, which is unity in faith and order, the unity of the Church and in the Church.

On December 7, 1965, after lengthy discussions in Rome and Constantinople, the Pope of Rome and the Ecumenical Patriarch issued a common declaration by which the reciprocal excommunications of 1054 were lifted.[5]

The mutual revocation of the 900-year-old excommunications by both churches drew unfavorable reactions from the Churches of Russia and Greece.

While in Manchester, I wrote my book *Orthodoxy, Roman Catholicism and Anglicanism* between the years 1964-1965, and, as I have said, it was published in 1972, with a few added notes relating to the progress of the negotiations which took place

---

[5] For the text, see my book *Orthodoxy, Roman Catholicism and Anglicanism* pp. 216-217. On the 25th anniversary of the lifting of the Anathemata, an evaluation of this significant event was written by Bartholomaios, Metropolitan of Chalcedon, now Ecumenical Patriarch, in *Epistimoniki Parousia*, a review of the Association of Graduates of Halki, Athens, 1991, pp. 105-113. It is fitting to mention here that after his elevation to the Ecumenical Throne, Patriarch Athenagoras sent a brotherly greeting to Pope Pius XII, but it remained unanswered.

before the start of the official dialogue between Roman Catholics and Orthodox. Though the future course of the dialogue was unknown, I made some observations which, as negotiations between the two parties went forward, proved to be correct. All my fears about the future of the dialogue are confirmed by Archbishop Stylianos of Australia, Co-President of the joint commission, as can be seen in his book *In the Margin of the Dialogue* (1980 – 1990), Athens, 1991.

In expressing my fears and hopes about the dialogue, I wrote, among other things:

> The commencement of the Dialogue on equal terms presupposes that the Roman church should give up claim of Primacy and be content with the thesis that her head, the Pope, should be *primus inter pares honoris causa*. But the Roman Church, in the Encyclical *Ecclesiam Suam*, continues to regard herself as the One church, insisting on the return of the 'separated brethren.'

Another very important obstacle to the Dialogue, as I wrote in my book, is the question of the Uniate Churches established within the jurisdictions of the Eastern Orthodox Churches with the aim of proselytizing the Orthodox faithful to Roman Catholicism. At the Rhodes Conference the Orthodox passed a resolution demanding of the Roman Church, as a precondition for the start of the dialogue, that she cease her propaganda and put an end to all her efforts to convert the Orthodox through the *Unia*. But as Archbishop Stylianos states, instead of disowning Uniatism, the Roman Church included in her Commission for the Dialogue eight Uniates, contrary to the agreement that Uniates would not participate in the deliberations of the Dialogue. It would be wrong to suppose that there were not some leading figures among the Roman Curia who could not see the facts as they stand. Cardinal Lercaro, at the time Archbishop of Bologna, in an address at the Greek Uniate College in Rome, called on the Roman Catholics to make an act of self-abasement and recognize that the Catholic Church is not yet entirely ready "to be looked at closely by the Orthodox," adding some points that are very applicable to the realities. He said, "We must once more reveal in its fullness the conciliar nature of the Church and realize its conciliarity in our ecclesiastical life. Only then can we proclaim officially to the Orthodox that we are prepared to respect in its full integrity one of the more impressive forms in which this conciliar spirit is expressed in the genuine traditions of the East, namely the institutions of the Patriarchate and the institutions of the autocephalous churches . . . Only then will it be possible to invite Eastern representatives to look closely at us."

From the Orthodox point of view the address of Cardinal Lercaro merits special consideration. Even today, does the Roman Church, as a whole, approve it? Cardinal Lercaro himself asked the whole Roman Catholic Church, both the leadership and the faithful, to adopt the right attitude towards the East, otherwise the symbolic gestures between Romans and Orthodox would be meaningless.

In my book *Greeks and Latins*, I state that the Greeks are still *papophiloi* but not *papodouloi*, by which I mean that we expect of the Roman Catholic Church a better understanding of the Orthodox Church; and that it cease invading the Orthodox Churches of Eastern Europe with the aim of re-establishing the Uniate Churches, re-united with the local Autocephalous Churches after World War II. This activity certainly constitutes a hindrance to the continuation of the Dialogue between the two Churches.

At any rate, the aforementioned book of Archbishop Stylianos presents this situation in a very gloomy light, particularly as it concerns the relations of Orthodoxy and Roman Catholicism.

I now turn our attention to the Oriental Churches, and will say that in spite of fifteen centuries of separation of the Oriental Orthodox Churches from the Orthodox Catholic Church, the identical ecclesiastical *phronema* prevails in both. This is the result of the meeting of the Inter-Orthodox Theological Committee for the Dialogue between the Eastern Orthodox and the Oriental Orthodox Churches held in Addis Ababa in 1971, a landmark in the efforts of these Churches to approach one another. However, of far from minor importance was the work of the two official Theological Sub-committees of the two families of the Eastern Church which met in Penteli (Athens) in 1973, and in Addis Ababa in 1975.

However, apart from the theological issues raised in contacts with the Orientals, there are other important factors which must be taken into account if the presuppositions for a full and well-balanced agreement between the Orthodox Catholic Church and the Oriental Orthodox Churches are to be met. These factors are the contacts between the leaders of both Churches, for they represent the mind of their respective Churches and supply the *consensus ecclesiae* in the theological discussions.

In my writings I have adopted the adjective "Orthodox" for the Orientals since they continue to live along with us, and for the simple reason that they are distinguished from us. For their part they do not deny our Orthodoxy; rather they disagree with the decisions of Holy Synods which condemned their church leaders such as Dioscorus, Severus, Timothy Aelurus and Philoxenus. They do not disagree with the dogmatic decisions of the four later Ecumenical Councils, some of which they recognize *de facto*. They do disagree with the procedures employed in the condemnation of their leaders who, in some ways, are our leaders as well.

In the extensive introductions, in English, to my books, *The Person of Jesus Christ in the Decisions of the Ecumenical Councils*, pp. 13-24, and *Movement towards Unity with the Oriental Orthodox Churches*, pp. 36-51, I examine the theological and ecclesiastical differences between the two families of Eastern Christendom and the prospects for reconciliation. I have taken into account the discussions in the four unofficial Theological Consultations between Eastern and Oriental Orthodox theologians, held at Aarhus (1964), Bristol (1967), Geneva (1970) and Addis Ababa (1970). Equally significant has been the work of the five unofficial consultations between theologians from the Oriental Orthodox Churches and the Roman Catholic Church, who met in Vienna in 1971, 1973, 1976, 1978 and 1988.

The outcome of all these unofficial consultations was the meeting of the Eastern Orthodox and Oriental Orthodox at the Anba Bishoy Monastery during 20-24 July 1989. Here an agreement was signed, whereby the Orthodox should lift the anathemas and condemnations against the Holy Synods of the Orthodox Orientals and their teacher, and that the Oriental Orthodox should do likewise with respect to the Holy Synods and the Fathers of the Orthodox Church, whom they have anathematized and condemned in the past.

Personally, I am struck by the fact that Photius the Great did not hesitate to communicate with the Armenians, although he appeared less lenient towards Dioscorus of Alexandria and Severus of Antioch. What needs to be added here is that both Churches, the Orthodox Catholic and the Roman Catholic, tried not so much to find common ground with the Orientals as to unite them with their Churches, in other words, how to compel them to submit to us, which was precisely our mistake.

In my opinion our first concern must be to resolve our differences with our brothers in the East, and then turn to the West with the aim with the aim of completing the task of ecclesiastical unity.

In any event, the last Joint Meeting in Geneva (23-28 September 1990) overcame all past hesitations, adopting the preparatory work of the Addis Ababa Meeting of 1971, which I had organized in my capacity of Archbishop of Aksum at that time. It proceeded to positive decisions, which must be implemented so that the dialogues may have practical implications and not end up as mere academic discussions.

It should not escape our attention that large Churches in these regions, with great vitality and long-standing history, have disappeared because they were isolated or spurned by other Churches and religions. I mention here as examples the churches of Nubia, Carthage, Arabia and Pentapolis.

I must again register my view regarding the Oriental Churches. It is my conviction that the various characterizations of these Churches – Ancient Lesser Churches, or Anti-Chalcedonian, or Pre-Chalcedonian – do not correspond to their true status. Therefore, I use the terms Eastern and Oriental, even though they are synonymous, and I am glad that in Addis Ababa in 1971, having suggested that the Orientals should also be called "Orthodox," that term was later adopted.

In making this suggestion to the Addis Ababa conference, it was my sense that we would be in harmony with the expression of St. John of Damascus when he said of Orientals: "They separated themselves from the Church on account of the Synod of Chalcedon, although in everything else they are Orthodox." (Having broken away from the Church because of the council of Chalcedon, they nevertheless remain Orthodox in other respects.)

Whether intentionally or in error, our authors often use the appellation "Orthodox" to denote local Churches of the Orientals. As I have stated elsewhere, and stress again here, the Orthodox Church is One, it is The Church; the Oriental Churches are local Churches distinct in that sense even from the Orthodox Churches. Union will remove their local status and they will become autocephalous Orthodox Churches. With us they will constitute the historic Church which produced the great Fathers; the Fathers who delineated the spiritual and synodical norms of the Church; the Fathers who founded the theological schools which remain venerable as having set the fundaments of our confession regarding the Person of our Lord Jesus Christ.

The initial theological formulations in the East contributed to the establishment of schools; these schools in turn share a common feature: they express the truth of the faith in the forms and terms of a spiritual synthesis. Thus the concept of ecclesiastical tradition developed differently from its Western counterpart. Whatever the perspective from which we examine the two forms of ecclesiastical tradition, Eastern and Western, we shall conclude that that of the East is richer, stronger, the mystical spirit within the Church dominated by faith.

While the Orthodox and the Roman Catholics preserved their unity more or less intact until the 15th century, what they could not preserve was their inner sense of fraternal existence because of deep divergence in the basic aspects of ecclesiastical ethos. By contrast the Orientals, although condemned by Ecumenical Synods, by remaining firmly within the Eastern spirit without wavering, attest to the stable forces that unite us. They have remained devoted to the sacramental and liturgical traditions, thus demonstrating our common origins and common pilgrimage.

As Greeks we have the brotherly duty to re-examine all those deviations in the doctrine of the Churches which exist to the present day under their respective names. Because at the time of their separation the leaders of the Church were Greeks, it is with the Greeks that they share a common tradition.[6] And this is precisely their complaint: that the Greek have not taken such action as would lead to our reunion with them.

More than any other Church, the Greeks have a unique connection with the Armenians, the Syrians, the Copts and the Ethiopians, though as the distinguished theologian cardinal Jean Daniélou rightly expressed it in a lecture he delivered in London,[7] Hellenism is the power which ignites the whole of the Christian Church.

Beyond the basic features of our common origins, our Oriental brethren have preserved intact the ecclesiastical structure to the extent that we are virtually identical in this dimension. In addition, they have so consciously adopted our customs as to be hardly distinguishable from us. They have maintained hieratic concepts and the patriarchal office at a high level of esteem, thus developing an ecclesiastical tradition that parallels our own. In turning favorably towards our Oriental brethren, we run no risk of encountering the innumerable Western innovations and modernizing views of other Churches; we shall be meeting the common inheritors of the Patriarchal Thrones of Alexandria and Antioch, sharing a common experience. For like us, they too have known the voracity of the Western

---

[6] The reader will be aware that the Annual *Abba Salama,* vols. 1-10, and the review *Ekklesiastikos Pharos,* vol. 51-61, contain ample information on the relations of these two families of the Eastern Church.

[7] *The Tablet,* 29 September 1951. Cf. also *The Church and the Hellenic Tradition,* in *Eastern Churches Quarterly,* 9, 1951, p. 175.

Churches, the methods, both licit and illicit that sought to adulterate Orthodox though, to wound our conscience and prestige through the Crusades, Uniatism, and divisive conversions achieved by long years of bribery and coercion.

Certainly political and economic pressures have rendered the Orthodox Catholic Church a captive of the West, which applies political models even in the ecclesiastical domain, so much so that Eastern Christianity seems incapable of studying its own problems, especially that which relates to its inner unity.

I believe that the Eastern Church continues to possess the treasure upon which the Western Church draws lavishly. But this treasure is the patrimony not only of the Greeks but of the Copts, the Ethiopians, the Armenians and the Syro-Jacobites as well.

The survival of the Coptic Church is a miracle, not only because it survived the brutal depredations of the Muslims, but because it managed to flourish within that oppressive regime. The genesis and growth of the Ethiopian Church, her salvation from the Roman Catholic missionary-troops; the preservation of her identity in spite of the stifling conditions surrounding her, indeed imposed on her by her enemies, represents a gigantic achievement of our faith in Africa. The survival of the Syro-Jacobite Church in Syria, and of the branch in India, is a phenomenon which astonishes the uniformed student of the history of our Church in these regions. Nor can we allow ourselves to overlook the unhappy vicissitudes of the Armenian Church, caused by atheists.

In these Churches it is faith in the *kenosis*, the humiliation of our Lord, which has prevailed as the enduring experience of the Church through the centuries.

Orthodoxy in Contemporary Europe

Metropolitan Methodios of Pisidia

Europe today, with a population of 500 million, continues to be under the influence of the main religious denominations: the Orthodox Churches, the Protestant Churches and the Roman Catholic Church.[1] Proportionally this influence does not correspond to the numbers of Eastern Church followers, the reason being that Protestants, though cut off from the Roman Catholic Church, remain under its influence. Even the Christian Socialist parties of the European countries cöoperate closely with Rome. For its part, Rome has a variety of methods and instrumentalities at her disposal to exercise her influence over all of Europe and to regulate the ecclesiastical life of all the people of Europe. There are the numerous monastic or-

[1] There are many who believe that Europe is no longer a Christian place. But a distinguished scholar, T. S. Elliot, in his book *The Unity of European Civilization*, reviewed in *Vema* for June 24, 1990, offers some additional interesting observations: "I am not so much interested in the common process as it relates to the Christian faithful of the present day. I speak rather of the common tradition of Christianity which formed Europe as it is today, and of the common elements of civilization which this shared Christian belief brought with it . . . The parliaments of Europe have their roots within Christianity. Even our thought is validated because it is grounded in Christianity. Only a Christian civilization could survive after the disappearance of the Christian. And I come to this conclusion not only because I am a Christian, but because I am a student of social biology."

ders; institutions of learning at all academic levels; diplomatic
missions in all the European capitals, making the presence of
the Roman Church felt in international organizations such as
the Council of Europe, the European Economic Commission
and the multiple services and committees of the United Nations Organization.

With all these mechanisms in place the Roman Catholic
Church has managed to make life problematic for other
Churches on the European continent. The statement of Rob-
ert Runcie, Archbishop of Canterbury, underscored the depth
of the problem when he said on October 1, 1989, "It is about
time for the sake of unity of the Church that the Pope of Rome
lead all Christians." This statement gives me pause, and I must
agree with G. Daratos' views on recent developments in Europe, expressed in his article published in the Athenian
newspaper *Vema*:[2] that the future of Europe is not played out
in Maastrich but in Rome. This is what Pope John Paul appeared to believe when he held an extraordinary Council of
Bishops in Rome, whose agenda was concerned with all the
countries of Eastern and Western Europe. Some 137 Bishops
took part in this Synod.

The main issue of the council was an analysis of the situation arising in Europe after the fall of the Communist regimes,
and the possibilities which now emerge for the return of all
peoples to the bosom of the Roman Church. The perception
of Pope John Paul II that Europe is one and undivided is well
known. It is a perception of a unity deeply rooted in Christianity. I am not sure that all the Orthodox Churches have
understood the Pope's intentions. I am sure, on the other hand,
that he has the Orthodox in mind and questions whether the
Greeks realize what the control of 500 million Europeans by
the Vatican means, for Europe and for them. Indeed I agree

[2] *Vema*, December 5, 1991.

with Daratos' observations that the new horizons for Catholicism which the Pope is opening in Europe do not pose a problem for the Orthodox Church, the Greek Church in particular. As I have stressed in my book, *Greeks and Latins*, (pp. 45 ff.) "we live at the end of the twentieth century and we are surrounded by the scene which Hellenism experienced from the Councils of 1274 in Lyons and of 1439 in Florence, when the Byzantine Emperor and the Ecumenical Patriarch went to Florence and participated in the Council held there."

From the East our friends the Turks exert pressure on us; from the West Rome flirts with us, while the Europeans appear once again to be needed. It is in such an atmosphere that we seek a safe route of escape. What might that be? If anyone has the answer, let him expound it to us. In soliciting an answer, I am not implying that I cannot answer the question myself. In fact my answer is readily found in the introduction to my recently published book (p. 17), where I state clearly why I ventured to write on the crisis in Hellenism and in the Church. It is a crisis reminiscent of those adventures of Byzantium during the 12th to the 15th centuries when the Greeks confronted fearful enemies, of the Empire and of Orthodoxy, and invariably turned to the West for military assistance. This utopian policy, of expecting protection from the West, proved to be a chimera, catastrophic for the continuity of the Byzantine Church and its society.

Our situation at that time is all too familiar to both older and contemporary thinkers, and in his article in *Vema*,[3] Mr. Marakis describes with clarity all the attempts of the Turks to infiltrate the entire Balkan Peninsula; their aim: to restore once again the Ottoman Empire and employing to this end, apart from Turkish diplomacy, the religious affinities which exist between some Moslem minorities in that region and the Is-

---

[3] Ibid., August 11, 1991.

lamic population of Turkey.

But when we speak of the "new world order" which was to follow the Persian Gulf War, we should be mindful not to see it in isolation from another "new world order," that which is envisioned in the activities of the Vatican State as depicted in the monumental Encyclical *Centicimus Annus*. The encyclical outlines the framework within which the Roman Church sees how this "new world order" must be established throughout Europe along with all that this inevitably implies.

Centicimus Annus followed close on the heels of the earlier *Slavorum Apostoli*, issued in 1985, by which the Pope acknowledged the work of the Greek Missionaries Cyril and Methodios, who had been sent to the Slavs by the Great Patriarch Photius. A distinguished Greek diplomat, N. Kavalouris, writing in the Athenian newspaper *Eleftherotypia*, offers a lengthy analysis of the prospect for the Vatican in today's Europe.[4] He writes, "Today, after the end of the ideological conflict between the capitalist West and the Communist East, the Pope realizes that he enjoys limitless freedom of action, without political restrictions such as he would have had to skirt during the first period of his pontificate. In *Centicimus Annus* he stressed the strength of the Church for the era of communism, of which as a Pole he had directed experience. In *Slavorum Apostoli* he projects mainly the Primacy of the Pope as complementing the great power of the United States. In *Centicimus Annus* Pope and Church are portrayed as a flexible Primacy vis-a-vis the United States, now, after the internal disintegration of the USSR, the only great power in the world. In this new state of affairs the Pope believes that, apart from a moral role, he is in position to play a major political and spiritual one.

The Pope's Encyclical Letter resonated strongly in the United States. Favorable comments by Richard John Newhouse

[4] *Eleftherotypia*, July 19, 1991.

appeared in the *Wall Street Journal* of May 3, 1991; the *Washington Post* and *The New York Times* also commented favorably.

Centicimus Annus is animated by an ecumenical spirit; it aims at safeguarding human dignity and argues support for those institutions which protect freedom and democracy. It looks not only to the Christianization of Europe, but also for eradicating the gap between rich and poor. Apart from explicitly religious and spiritual concerns, it expresses the multiple dimensions of Vatican policy; it lays down a code of discipline which bears directly on the outlook of the European Community towards the countries of Eastern Europe.

In keeping with this policy the Pope supports the Council of Europe (CCEE) in its aim to encourage more frequent contacts between East and West. Since 1980, the council of Bishops has the initiative for setting up a Commission of the Episcopates of the European Community (COMECE). This Commission will specialize in matters of cöoperation with agencies of the European Community. Based on the experience of it members, the Commission supports the cöoperation of the two organizations for a better understanding of all Christians on the European Continent.

On March 3, 1980, the first President of COMECE, Msgr. Hengsbach, made the following statement to the Press Agency of France: "Every European country which is ruled by a democratic constitution, which is in line with the demands of the Treaty of Rome, should soon enter the Community." He then visited the Fourth Committee of the European Community in Brussels. After his meeting with Dejanie on matters of development, and with Degemb on issues of employment, he met with the President of the Commission, Mr. Thorn. Later, on the 19th and 20th of June, 1985, in Brussels, COMECE cöoperated with the new President, Jacques Dellor, on questions affecting the future of the Commission, and on December 2, 1986, they discussed the subject of the intentions of Islam.

The activity of the Pope is in line with the beliefs of Jacques Dellor with regard to Catholicism and his endeavors for European unity. This is the opinion of Professor Hoffman of Harvard University as expressed in an article in the newspaper *The European Community* (1991). Professor Hoffman says that Jacques Dellor disposes and composes Christian democracy and socialism, a composition on which the European Community is structured.

In an article that appeared in the newspaper *Sunday Correspondent* of May 17, 1990, under the caption "Europe United and Divided," written with reference to the Encyclical Letter *Populorum Progressio* (dated March 26, 1967) of Pope Paul VI, Jacques Dellor, among other comments, says, "Development is the new name for Peace."[5] It should be said here that the General Secretariat of the Commission of Bishops of the European Community (COMECE) maintains frequent contacts with some services of the European Community on commercial, social, political and humanistic problems that come under the program of the COMECE.[6]

As I have said, the European Community and the Roman Church do not overlook Europe's obligations towards the Third World. This is attested to by Jacques Dellor as well as the Encyclical *Centicimus Annus*.

What is the position of the Orthodox Church in the new Europe? No one can answer this question based on concrete data. Orthodox interest is on the part of individuals. An example may be seen in the scholarly work of Emeritus Professor

---

[5] Cf. a brief of this article of Jacques Dellor in the newspaper *Kathimerine*, June 3, 1990.
[6] Cf. E. Theodorou, *The Spiritual Foundations of Europe*, in the magazine *Ecclesia*, June 1, 1990, pp. 289-292.

A. Fytrakis entitled, *The Position and the Mission of the Greek Orthodox Church in Western Europe Today* (Athens 1984). It is this author's view that thus far nothing has been done that could be seen as a broad program of the whole body of the Orthodox Churches in Europe. He regards the observations of distinguished men of letters as irrelevant for the masses of European society; nor do they influence the political agendas of governments as they define the lives of their peoples.

Unfortunately, the Greek Orthodox Church has not succeeded in extending her influence on the citizens of those countries among whom she lives; nor indeed has she had any influence on the social process in Greece, a fact that we must not conceal.

We have not had access to deliberations either in Greece or in Europe. As a consequence the Greek spirit speaks with a very weak voice in the present day.

It is the witness of history, and the consensus of all who have studied European society, that Europe as a whole, Eastern and Western, is founded on Greco-Roman classical learning and Christianity; in the countries of Eastern Europe in particular the immense contribution of Hellenic Christianity is an indisputable fact, acknowledged by all the faithful of these countries. But today the Greek spiritual and ecclesiastical voice is weak, so much so that Dirozel dared to declare recently that the Greeks should not be admitted to the European Union because they are descendants of Turks![7] This means that there

---

[7] In addition to Dirozel, the Englishman Woodhouse has also disputed the direct descendance of the present-day Greek from the ancient Greeks. Cf. the Athenian newspaper *Ethnos* of July 8, 1991, on the negligence of the Greeks in not preventing the publication of J.B. Dirozel's work, and a special article by Professor M. Andronicos: *The Other Side of History* in the Newspaper *Vema*, June 2, 1990. It confirms my own views about this negligence. See further what is said by Jean-Pierre Vernant in his article, *There are*

is no objection if it is recognized that our forefathers were the
very leaven of European civilization. Before the fall of
Constantinople we formed the basis of Italian and European
civilization. Our question is: who are the contemporary spiritual and political men? For if their voices carried beyond
Greece's frontiers, I am sure that no anti-Hellene or mis-
Hellene would dare express such monstrous views.[8] Should
these poisonous ideas persist and become part of the common
political "paideia" which the European Community will impose on all its member nations, then along with this "paideia"
Orthodoxy itself will be displaced. We must be mindful of the
fact that the spirit of phil-hellenism flourished in Europe before the establishment of the independent Greek State.
According to G. Kremos (1890), after the independence of
Greece, we observe a decline in the State and the society.

We are experiencing today what A. Koraes once foretold:
we are beggars in everything.

Borrowings from foreigners, or to put it more plainly, bread-

Many Stories, in *Vema*, June 3, 1990. A lengthy article on the same
subject appeared in the newspaper *Orthodox Typos* for May 23,
1990, under the caption *Contemporary Violence*. Cf. the article of E.
Theodorou, *Hellenism and the European History* in *Eleftheros Typos*,
April 19, 1990; M. Ploritis, *The Mysteries of Brussels: Questions and
Conclusions about the Unhistoric History*, in *Vema*, September 2,
1990; S. Alexiou, *With Simple Logic, What Did We Do?*, in
Kathimerini, May 3, 1990; P. Petrides, *The European History of
Europe and its Enduring Contribution: Hellenism, An Inexhaustible
Spring of Idea*, in *Ethnos*, May 9, 1990. In *Kathimerini* for May #,
1990, a number of articles appeared under the following the titles:
Who Snatched our Europe?; *The History of Europe*; *Too Much for
Nothing*; *New and Unknown Elements in the Much Discussed Book*;
The Complete Table of Contents, etc.

[8] I plan to make a special study of this subject, to be written in
one of the European languages.

borrowings of words and phrases of which all the stores of language are full. Along with the dishonor there is absolute ignorance and honor from idiots … What is the profit in knowing the language of others when he who knows it takes not what is correct, but merely distorts and deforms his own language?

It is my opinion that these thoughts of Koraes describe the present condition of Greek society, preventing it from participating in the European structures. It is impossible for another reason. Suppose there are persons who have both the desire and the ability to do something for Greece and for Orthodoxy; they are frustrated in their efforts because there are always incapable people standing in their way who, in company with others of malicious intent, connive against the national and ecclesiastical Greek interests.

There is something further to consider. It is the religious factor, which is not a strong feature of Europeans. For example; In Denmark only 15% of the people have any interest in religion; in France 14%; 28% in Germany; 25% in Great Britain; 59% in Italy; 55% in Spain. The Roman Catholic influence is evident in the higher percentages for Catholic countries. In a small book entitled *Europe: A Small Compilation of Texts* (Athens 1977), which refers to the "Week of Europe," May 5-16, 1976, all the contributors, Greeks and non-Greeks alike, express the view that Christianity is a precious element of the European in a united Europe as many have dreamed of it since 1255, i.e. from the time of Philip the Handsome of France to Kountehove-Kalergi, who lived in the period between the First and Second World Wars and is the founder of "Paneurope."[9]

---

[9] In *Kathimerini* for April 20, 1990, there is an enlightening series of essays dealing with the actual founders of United Europe under these titles: *Who United Europe?*; *The Current Leaders of the European Community Are Not the First Who Sacked (sic) This*; *But*

When we speak of the Christian element as precious for the unity of Europe, which element do we mean? Which Christianity do they have in mind when we consider the numerous protracted and catastrophic religious wars in Europe, when we remember how often the Christian East faced invasion by armies trained and sent against her by European Christian countries?

History is being repeated today with the invasion of Roman Catholic bishops into the Eastern countries. This behavior of the Roman Church poisons relations between Orthodox and Roman Catholics in those countries. They have made incursions not only into regions where there are Uniates, but even into Moscow. Such conduct on Rome's part hampers any cöoperation of the Churches aimed at the re-evangelization of Europe, indeed conveys the impression that the consolidation of Christian life in a united Europe is the exclusive concern of the Roman Catholic Church. It is very important that Orthodox officials from Moscow should meet with Vatican representatives in Geneva in March, 1992. When Germany recognizes the independence of many local States enjoying Vatican favor, there can be no doubt about Rome's intentions to bring all of Christian Europe under her complete hegemony.

Because of recent undesirable events in the Eastern countries, the Orthodox church today does not participate in the Convention of the Bishops of Europe organized by the Vatican. In my estimation, however, this attitude on the part of the Orthodox Church will neither alter the process in the Roman Catholic Church nor hinder her in realizing her program.

Thus the question this raises for us is: Have *we* any pro-

There Is Doubt that Charlemagne Is the Founder of Euro-Latin-Europe. Cf. M. Roushel *Charlemagne the Founder of Europe*, in *History*, Part 282 (1991), pp. 35-43.

gram? What are *we* going to do? Unfortunately, owing to the lack of unity among the Orthodox Churches, our side presents an unpromising picture. It should not escape our attention that in each Orthodox Church there are particular preferences which soon become apparent. I believe that unity of the Autocephalous Churches requires a common approach transcending national and ecclesiastical interests, which none is ready to sacrifice. The fact is well attested by examples that may be drawn from the recent past and from current happenings.

There is no alternative for the Orthodox Churches but to take a common line concerning their policy in Europe. This is all that is possible for them, if they hope to counter the aims of the Catholic Church, namely to impose her Imperium on the whole of Europe. Such an initiative of a united Orthodox Church will compel the Catholic Church to cöoperate on equal terms for peace, progress and democracy in Europe as a whole.[10] The Greek Churches and the Churches of Eastern Europe must hasten to understand that they have been encircled by Skopja, Albania, Croatia, Slovenia, Austria, Hungary, Czecho-slovakia and Poland; and that their position has been undermined by the Uniates who have taken root in their very bosom. It is time the Russian Orthodox Church came to the realization that unilateral intercommunion with Rome, which occurred some years ago in Rome, and her private theological discussions with the Evangelicals in Germany, have proven to be entirely unprofitable for her.[11]

---

[10] The Intellectual and former Minister St. Papathemelis in an article in *Vema*, May 20, 1990, entitled *The Ecumenical Patriarchate vis-à-vis International Developments: Phanari, Greece, Europe,* indicates the reasons which prevent the Ecumenical Patriarchate from leading Orthodoxy and involving itself in European affairs.

[11] Another member of the Greek Parliament, Basil Papadopoulos, in three articles entitled: *Orthodoxy Facing the Year 2000: A Politician Makes Accusations and Proposals for Orthodoxy,* in *Nike,*

The Orthodox Churches must avoid appearing in Europe in a negative light. They must present themselves as a well-constituted body, as sister Churches in harmony and close cöoperation with leading officials of the European Communities; they will thus be able to safeguard the Orthodox ethos and advance those attributes and characteristics as they are lived by Christian European peoples.

At this time, the Russian Orthodox Church, as a sister to the other Orthodox Churches, has emerged as a powerful Church in Europe. What will happen should she regain her role as defender of European civilization? Will she rise as the spiritual force of Russia as in the time of Peter the Great and assume the role of sequel to the Byzantine Empire and perhaps the third Rome? What will happen should Russia resume her former role in Europe? A deeply Christian country will be very important to the stability of Europe. And this because, as I have said, Europe is substantially an idea born out of the union of two powerful elements – the legacy of the classical world and Medieval Christianity. Of the confluence of these two streams Russia is the primary heir, then comes Germany.[12]

It is not for me to point out the serious shortcomings of our Church as she confronts present-day challenges. These have been underscored by many others who generally lament our social, ecclesiastical and spiritual bankruptcy. One is the late Greek T. Lignadis, who has raised such questions in his book entitled *I Collapse*. Meanwhile the Greek newspapers carry daily desperate complaints about the crisis of morality, urging the need for vigilance.

December 11, 12, and Orthodox Churches, as well as other issues.
[12] Cf. k. P. Kalligas, *The Rise of Russianism: Russia Rediscovers Itself after the Disappearance of the "Painting' and Emerges from Pre-history*, in *Kathimerini*, July 7, 1991.

I come now to another point which I mentioned at the beginning. We must emphasize Christian Democratic countries, i.e. those that are governed by Christian Democratic parties and where Catholicism is the dominant element (Holland being somewhat differentiated). But Christian Democratic parties exist in other countries as well, as in Yugoslavia, Romania, Bulgaria, Estonia and Lithuania. Although Europe will not necessarily become more Christian, she will facilitate the approach to the Vatican; at the present time Christian Democratic parties are political rather than Christian as they were in the past. Thus the Greek Church must choose close cöoperation with the Russian Church and the rest of the churches of Eastern Europe. However, I do not see this as feasible, given the grandiose vision the Russian Church has of herself.

Here it must be noted that after the Communist Revolution in Russia, a great number of Russian Orthodox thinkers and theologians left their country to find refuge in Western Europe. Persons like N. Berdayev, S. Bulgakov, G. Florovsky, V. Lossky, L. Ouspensky, L. Zander, A. Schmemann, J. Meyendorff. N. Zernov and many others contributed immensely to the impact of the Orthodox faith on the Western world. In spite of the difficulties they faced as refugees, the Russian Orthodox people in Western Europe established in Paris the well known Seminary of St. Sergius under the jurisdiction of the Ecumenical Patriarchate and, after the Second World War, in 1950 began publishing the bilingual review *Messager de l'Exarchat du Patriarche Russen Europe Occidentale*, (Nouvelle Series).

Today the Russian Orthodox are attuned to the political changes in the East and will follow their political leaders in advancing the piety and splendor we associate with the greatness of Russian Orthodoxy. Thus far, however, the Europeans have been merely spectators to the regeneration of Christianity in Russia, Ukraine and Byelorussia, expressing their admiration for the survival of Christianity under such a tyrannical social system. It is too early to make any prophecy as to what the Russians will do within the European community, which ultimately will embrace the aforementioned countries.

One must not forget what Dostoyevsky wrote at the height of his wisdom, though at the threshold of death; "Europe is a mother to us, as is Russia, she is our Mother; we have taken much from her and shall do so again, and we do not wish to be ungrateful to her." His last hope was Messianism, but a Messianism that grew out of his perception of Russia as a sort of idealized Europe which was called upon to save and renew Europe.

Today Russian theologians believe that "all the best that Russia has created is the result of the inward reconciliation of 'Eastern' and 'Western,' of all that was true and immortal that sprouted from Byzantine seed, but could grow only by identifying itself once more with the general history of Christian humanity."[13] This suffices to explain our reservations over the role which Russian Orthodoxy will play in coming European affairs.

G. Saridakis, a Greek member of the European Parliament, in an article which appeared in the Athenian newspaper *Kathemerine* of July 26, 1990, referring to the presentation of Greek civilization, expresses a number of important perceptions relating to our Orthodox Church. Inter alia he writes: "To seek for all the peoples of the European Continent a contemporary identity is an urgent necessity and will likely result in some dramatic revelations after the recent developments in Central and Eastern Europe."

[13] A. Schmemann, *Historical Road of Eastern Orthodoxy*, Translated by L. W. Kesich, *St. Vladimir's Seminary Press*, New York, 1977, p. 338.

The role of the Christian Church (that of the Orthodox Church is, unfortunately of lesser importance) in these developments demonstrates that non-material virtues occupy no significant place in the composition of that emerging identity, in spite of the attraction to them which the emerging society found in them at the outset.

There is a great risk of a pseudo-renaissance. Only by injecting the authentic values of the Greek spirit can the rising renaissance be deflected from deviating into commercialism, which would be its undoing.

G. Saridakis poses the question, "What must we do?" And he himself gives the reply; "We must reconstitute the unity of the ancient Greek spirit, melding Orthodox Byzantium and contemporary Greek society in the areas of thought, of letters and of science." Further he proposes the establishment of a high-level Academy of Philosophy and Mathematics. (It appears that Mr. Saridakis is unaware that such an academy for the Greeks abroad was founded by me as Archbishop of Thyateira and Great Britain in February of 1988.[14] Those who followed Church developments in that year will have known the reasons which hindered that Academy from materializing and functioning.) Mr. Saridakis proposes the establishment of two European Institutions of Greek Christianity, one in Brussels and one in Prague or Moscow; and later two more, one in the United States and another in Japan.

In his article Mr. Saridakis shares more and more interesting insights into the propagation of Orthodoxy and Greek civilization in Europe. In particular he stresses the responsibility of those Greeks who work in relevant agencies of the European Commission and concludes: "If we do not adopt, as

---

[14] Cf. *A Symposium for the Greek Woman Abroad* held in London, January 1-2, 1988, Athens, 1988, edited by E. Mexis.

soon as possible, the objective 'Greece, Universal Spiritual Power,' we shall have put ourselves outside the 'predetermined' historic theses."

Unfortunately, the Greeks are absorbed only in the past; they are either indifferent to or unable to follow current developments, because they demand actions that are self-explanatory. It is good to write books, but this is an inadequate exercise; books do not make history. I offer this example: We founded the institute for Byzantine Studies in Venice when there are many similar, independent institutes within the departments of various Universities throughout the world.

The fact is that we are not engaged with urgent problems, so I am afraid that, as Orthodox, we have missed the train that goes to Europe. In the end we shall be obliged to tolerate the actions of the Uniates unless, as I have said earlier, Russia has its ecclesiastical *perestroika* and appears in Europe under such leadership. In that event Europeans will make their accommodation with her and the Greeks will ultimately remain outside the process of Europe's transformation.